death poems

Classic, Contemporary, Witty, Serious, Tear-Jerking,
Wise, Profound, Angry, Funny, Spiritual, Atheistic,
Uncertain, Personal, Political, Mythic, Earthy,
and Only Occasionally Morbid

Edited by Russ Kick

disinformation®

12+
7-16

Published by Disinformation Books,
an imprint of Red Wheel/Weiser, LLC

with offices at
665 Third Street, Suite 400
San Francisco, CA 94107
www.redwheelweiser.com

Library of Congress Cataloging-in-Publication Data

Death Poems : classic, contemporary, witty, serious, tear-jerking, wise, profound, angry, funny, spiritual, atheistic, uncertain, personal, political, mythic, earthy, and only occasionally morbid / edited by Russ Kick.

    pages cm

    ISBN 978-1-938875-04-5

    1. Death--Poetry. I. Kick, Russell, editor of compilation.
    PN6110.D4D43 2013
    808.81'93548--dc23   2013026737

Cover design by Jim Warner
Interior by Kathryn Sky-Peck

See pages 324–327 for credits and permissions.

Printed in the United States of America
WOR
10 9 8 7 6 5 4 3 2 1

Disinformation® is a registered trademark of The Disinformation Company Ltd.

The paper used in this publication meets the minimum requirements of the American National Standard for Information Sciences—Permanence of Paper for Printed Library Materials Z39.48-199.

Contents

introduction

Every poem [is] an epitaph.

T.S. ELIOT

Name any well-known poet from any age, any country. He or she wrote at least one poem about death, most likely several poems. I can basically guarantee it. Death is one of the most common themes in the entirety of poetry. Whether it's a lamentation for a loved one or a public figure, a reflection on their own upcoming appointment with the grave, a meditation on the nature of death, or perhaps what happens afterward, every poet has found inspiration—sometimes welcome, often not—in the fate we all have in common. It provides a lens through which to examine life, changing everything else by its looming, inevitable presence. Our time here is brief; this play has a limited engagement, and there are no do-overs. Everything we do counts. Time is always running out, and the poets know that this casts life in an entirely different light than if we were immortal.

Death also provides a profound mystery—the ultimate mystery, really—to be examined, prodded, hypothesized about, potentially unraveled (but probably not). Poets love a mystery, and there is none bigger. In an interview, the great Anne Sexton said: "You see, I can explain sex in a minute, but death—I can't explain."

Finally, death provides a taboo, which poets love. It's disturbing, not to be talked about. But poetry specializes in taboos. It provides a way to speak about the unspeakable. The social rules of normal discourse, even the social rules of other types of writing, don't apply to poetry. By approaching things obliquely, by using language in a nonordinary—you could even say "magic"—way, by short-circuiting the rules of dialog and sneaking underneath the barbed wire of our rational, logical minds, poetry can address with impunity any topic it wants to. "Tell all the Truth," Emily Dickinson wrote, "but tell it slant."

Given the universality of death in poetry, you would expect to find a lot of anthologies collecting poetry on the topic. Themed collections of poetry are extremely popular. Bookshelves sag with anthologies of cowboy poetry, Japanese poetry, poems about the ocean, poems on motherhood, baseball, spirituality, music, food. . . . The number of books that collect love poetry is beyond calculating. And, as I write this, you can choose from more than *ten* anthologies of dog poetry in print. (Cats have around the same number.) But no one has brought together a big selection of the wide-ranging poems about death. There are several anthologies of poems specifically about loss, mourning, and grieving, and some of them are specifically marketed as providing readings for funeral services, or as a way to help the bereaved cope with their loss. There is a small omnibus of poems about murder, and you won't have trouble finding anthologies of war poems.

Just why it has been mostly ignored is puzzling, but my guess is that the taboo of death comes into play here. Maybe it strikes publishers and anthologists as morose. Maybe the topic of death is considered too much of a buzzkill. Putting together anthologies about personal loss and grieving is a psychological service. Creating anthologies about war is an historical and social service. But creating an anthology about death in general—in all its aspects—well, that's just bleak, right? Morbid. No, actually. Not at all. When you have many of the finest creative minds in history addressing one of the most important aspects of the human condition, you're going to get riches—a revealing, finely wrought kaleidoscope of ideas, attitudes, and experiences.

You're going to get Walt Whitman celebrating death as an important part of the richness of life. Lord Byron penning a beautiful epitaph for his beloved dog (there's dogs and poetry again!). Emily Dickinson going for a carriage ride with Death, and Dylan Thomas pleading with his father to not go gentle into that good night. The ancient Greek playwright Aeschylus ironically but accurately noting death's role as a healer. The Nobel Prize-winning Modernist poet Wallace Stevens opining that "Death is the mother of beauty." The decadent Charles Baudelaire reminding his lover that one day she'll be a rotting corpse. Thomas Hardy—best known for his novels *Tess of the d'Urbervilles* and *The Mayor of Casterbridge*—wryly writing about a widow and an ex-wife meeting over the grave of the man they had in common. American slaves singing of the holy glories to come, and the Irish singing about a man who comes back to life at his own wake. The ancient Indian holy text *The Baghavad Gita* explaining the immortality of our true essence. Biting epitaphs by Scotland's Robert Burns. Wanda Coleman's furious litany of innocent African Americans killed by police.

In this collection, several soldier-poets write of life in the trenches and on the battlefield, and Miranda Beeson offers an unexpected angle on 9/11. Former US Poet Laureate Billy Collins cheekily wonders if death is closing in on him, while an earlier Laureate, William Stafford, writes about losing his grip while mountain climbing. The seventeenth-century Cavalier poet Robert Herrick ponders the death of trees, and, around 250 years later, Imagist poet Amy Lowell graphically describes killing flowers. Literary legend D.H. Lawrence uses the moon to form a pact with his dead beloved, while the always astonishing Edna St. Vincent Millay is relieved that her paramour died before their relationship could go sour. The recently departed Lucille Clifton addresses the unborn child she aborted at home, while Charlotte Brontë grieves for her younger sister Anne, killed by consumption. Todd Davis puts a rabbit out of its misery, and Linda Hogan comforts a horse who has lost her foal. Two of the poets here (Tichborne and Villon) wrote verse while waiting for their death sentence the following morning. Others imagine what Heaven or Hell might be like. Some poets can't wait to die, while the unjustly overlooked Sara Teasdale loves life and nature so much that she doesn't want to leave, even vowing to find a way back.

As you can tell, this collection ranges dramatically. It goes across all of history, from the ancients straight through to today. Across countries and languages, across schools of poetry. You'll find a plethora of approaches—witty, humorous, deadly serious, tear-jerking, wise, profound, angry, spiritual, atheistic, uncertain, highly personal, political, mythic, earthy, and only occasionally morbid. Every angle you can think of is covered—the deaths of children, lost loves, funeral rites, close calls, eating meat, serial killers, the death penalty, roadkill, the Underworld, reincarnation, elegies for famous people, death as an equalizer, death as a junk man, death as a child, the death of God, the death of death . . .

This is a dazzling, largely unmined vein in poetry's long history. I hope this collection captures a big cross section of that mosaic.

—RUSS KICK

the nature of death

In which the poets reflect on what death is, meditate on why it happens, and pontificate on what it means to us

From "Song of Myself"

WALT WHITMAN

I wish I could translate the hints about the dead young men and women,
And the hints about old men and mothers, and the offspring taken soon
    out of their laps.
What do you think has become of the young and old men?
And what do you think has become of the women and children?

They are alive and well somewhere,
The smallest sprout shows there is really no death,
And if ever there was it led forward life, and does not wait at the end to
    arrest it,
And ceas'd the moment life appear'd.

All goes onward and outward, nothing collapses,
And to die is different from what any one supposed, and luckier.

• • •

Death the Leveller

JAMES SHIRLEY

The glories of our blood and state
    Are shadows, not substantial things;
There is no armour against fate;
    Death lays his icy hand on kings:
        Sceptre and Crown
        Must tumble down,
And in the dust be equal made
With the poor crookèd scythe and spade.

Some men with swords may reap the field,
    And plant fresh laurels where they kill:
But their strong nerves at last must yield;
    They tame but one another still:

Early or late
They stoop to fate,
And must give up their murmuring breath,
When they, pale captives, creep to death.

The garlands wither on your brow;
  Then boast no more your mighty deeds;
Upon Death's purple altar now
  See, where the victor-victim bleeds:
    Your heads must come
    To the cold tomb;
Only the actions of the just
Smell sweet, and blossom in their dust.

• • •

Dirge

ALFRED KREYMBORG

Death alone
has sympathy for weariness:
understanding
of the ways
of mathematics:
of the struggle
against giving up what was given:
the plus one minus one
of nitrogen for oxygen:
and the unequal odds,
you a cell
against the universe,
a breath or two
against all time:
Death alone
takes what is left
without protest, criticism

or a demand for more
than one can give
who can give
no more than was given:
doesn't even ask,
but accepts it as it is,
without examination,
valuation,
or comparison.

· · ·

Poets Have Chanted Mortality

JOHN CROWE RANSOM

It had better been hidden
    But the Poets inform:
We are chattel and liege
    Of an undying Worm.

Were you, Will, disheartened,
    When all Stratford's gentry
Left their Queen and took service
    In his low-lying country?

How many white cities
    And grey fleets on the storm
Have proud-builded, hard-battled,
    For this undying Worm?

Was a sweet chaste lady
    Would none of her lover.
Nay, here comes the Lewd One,
    Creeps under her cover!

Have ye said there's no deathless
    Of face, fashion, form,
Forgetting to honor
    The extent of the Worm?

O ye laughers and light-lipped,
    Ye faithless, infirm,
I can tell you who's constant,
    'Tis the Eminent Worm.

Ye shall trip on no limits,
    Neither time ye your term,
In the realms of His Absolute
    Highness the Worm.

•   •   •

Death Is a Fisherman

BENJAMIN FRANKLIN (ATTRIBUTED)

Death is a fisherman, the world we see
His fish-pond is, and we the fishes be;
His net some general sickness; howe'er he
Is not so kind as other fishers be;
For if they take one of the smaller fry,
They throw him in again, he shall not die:
But death is sure to kill all he can get,
And all is fish with him that comes to net.

•   •   •

Death Snips Proud Men

CARL SANDBURG

Death is stronger than all the governments because
       the governments are men and men die and then
       death laughs: Now you see 'em, now you don't.

Death is stronger than all proud men and so death
       snips proud men on the nose, throws a pair of
       dice and says: Read 'em and weep.

Death sends a radiogram every day: When I want
       you I'll drop in—and then one day he comes with a
       master-key and lets himself in and says: We'll go now.

Death is a nurse mother with big arms: 'Twon't hurt
       you at all; it's your time now; just need a
       long sleep, child; what have you had anyhow
       better than sleep?

• • •

On Death, Without Exaggeration

WISLAWA SZYMBORSKA

It can't take a joke,
find a star, make a bridge.
It knows nothing about weaving, mining, farming,
building ships, or baking cakes.

In our planning for tomorrow,
it has the final word,
which is always beside the point.

It can't even get the things done
that are part of its trade:
dig a grave,
make a coffin,
clean up after itself.

Preoccupied with killing,
it does the job awkwardly,
without system or skill.
As though each of us were its first kill.

Oh, it has its triumphs,
but look at its countless defeats,
missed blows,
and repeat attempts!

Sometimes it isn't strong enough
to swat a fly from the air.
Many are the caterpillars
that have outcrawled it.

All those bulbs, pods,
tentacles, fins, tracheae,
nuptial plumage, and winter fur
show that it has fallen behind
with its halfhearted work.

Ill will won't help
and even our lending a hand with wars and coups d'état
is so far not enough.

Hearts beat inside eggs.
Babies' skeletons grow.
Seeds, hard at work, sprout their first tiny pair of leaves
and sometimes even tall trees fall away.

Whoever claims that it's omnipotent
is himself living proof
that it's not.

There's no life
that couldn't be immortal
if only for a moment.

Death
always arrives by that very moment too late.

In vain it tugs at the knob
of the invisible door.
As far as you've come
can't be undone.

Translated from the Polish by Stanislaw Barańczak and Clare Cavanagh

• • •

That Morning

STANLEY MOSS

I got up a little after daybreak:
I saw a Luna Moth had fallen
between the window and a torn screen.
I lifted the window, the wings broke
on the floor, became green and silver powder.
My eyes followed green, as if all green
was a single web, past the Lombardy poplars,
and the lilac hedge leading to the back road.
I can believe the world
might have been the color of hide or driftwood,

but there was—and is—the gift of green,
and a second gift we can perceive the green,
although we are often blind to miracles.
There was no resurrection of green and silver wings.
They became a blue stain on an oak floor.
I wish I had done something ordinary,
performed an unknown, unseen miracle,
raised the window the night before,
let the chill November air come in.

I cannot help remembering
e.e. cummings' wife said, hearing him
choking to death in the next room,
she thought she heard moths on the window screen
attracted to the nightlight in his study.
Reader, my head is not a gravestone.
It's just that a dead poet and a Luna Moth
alighted. Mr. Death, you're not a stone wall.
You're more like a chain-link fence
I can see through to the other side. There's the rub:
You are a democracy, the land of opportunity,
the Patria. Some say you are a picnic.
Are there any gate-crashers beside the barbecue?
I'm afraid every living and once-living thing
will be asked to leave again.
The first death is just playtime.
There is a DEAD END beyond darkness
where everyone and every thing tries to turn around.
Every thing that ever lived sounds its horn.
And you, Mr. Death, are just a traffic cop.

• • •

"Death is a dialogue between"

EMILY DICKINSON

Death is a dialogue between
The spirit and the dust.
"Dissolve," says Death. The Spirit, "Sir,
I have another trust."

Death doubts it, argues from the ground.
The Spirit turns away,
Just laying off, for evidence,
An overcoat of clay.

• • •

Death

GEORGE PELLEW

Calm Death, God of crossed hands and passionless eyes,
Thou God that never heedest gift nor prayer,
Men blindly call thee cruel, unaware
That everything is dearer since it dies.
Worn by the chain of years, without surprise,
The wise man welcomes thee, and leaves the glare
Of noisy sunshine gladly, and his share
He chose not in mad life and windy skies.
Passions and dreams of love, the fever and fret
Of toil, seem vain and petty when we gaze
On the imperious Lords who have no breath:
Atoms or worlds—we call them lifeless, yet
In thy unending peaceful day of days
They are divine, all-comprehending Death.

• • •

Faded Love

BARRY GIFFORD

I am surrounded by death
it happens to everyone
all the time
Some people try not to notice
not me I've always known this
and paid attention
Nobody forces me to go on
I know what this means
one day I won't pay attention
and nobody will notice

. . .

From *Queen Mab*

PERCY BYSSHE SHELLEY

How wonderful is Death,
  Death, and his brother Sleep!
One, pale as yonder waning moon
  With lips of lurid blue;
  The other, rosy as the morn
When throned on ocean's wave
  It blushes o'er the world;
Yet both so passing wonderful!

. . .

Morphine

HEINRICH HEINE

Great is the similarity between
These two fair figures, although one appears
Much paler than the other, far more calm;
Fairer and nobler even, I might say,
Than his companion, in whose arms
I lay so warmly. How divine and soft
Were all his smiles, and what a look was his!
It must have been the poppy-wreath he wore
About his brows that touched my throbbing head
And with its magic perfume soothed all pain
And sorrow in my soul . . . But such sweet balm
Lasts but a little while; I can be cured
Completely only when the other one,
The grave and paler brother, drops his torch.
For Sleep is good, but Death is better still—
The best is never to be born at all.

Translated from the German by Louis Untermeyer

• • •

On Death

JOHN KEATS

Can death be sleep, when life is but a dream,
And scenes of bliss pass as a phantom by?
The transient pleasures as a vision seem,
And yet we think the greatest pain's to die.

How strange it is that man on earth should roam,
And lead a life of woe, but not forsake
His rugged path; nor dare he view alone
His future doom which is but to awake.

• • •

Sleep and His Brother Death

WILLIAM HAMILTON HAYNE

Just ere the darkness is withdrawn,
  In seasons of cold or heat,
Close to the boundary line of Dawn
  These mystical brothers meet.

They clasp their weird and shadowy hands,
  As they listen each to each,
But never a mortal understands
  Their strange immortal speech.

• • •

From *The Faerie Queene*

EDMUND SPENSER

For all that lives, is subject to that law:
All things decay in time, and to their end do draw.

• • •

"Were I a King"

EDWARD VERE, EARL OF OXFORD

Were I a King, I might command content;
  Were I obscure, unknown should be my cares;
And were I dead, no thoughts should me torment,—
  Nor words, nor wrongs, nor love, nor hate, nor fears!
  A doubtful choice for me, of three things, one to crave:
    A Kingdom, or a Cottage, or a Grave!

• • •

Death the Consecrator

CAROLINE SPENCER

O Death, the Consecrator!
Nothing so sanctifies a name
As to be written—Dead.
Nothing so wins a life from blame,
So covers it from wrath and shame,
As doth the burial-bed.

O Death, the revelator!
Our deepest passions never move
Till thou hast bid them wake;
We know not half how much we love
Till all below and all above
Is shrouded for our sake.

O Death, the great peacemaker!
If enmity hath come between
There's naught like death to heal it;
And if we love, O priceless pain,
O bitter-sweet, when love is vain!
There's naught like death to seal it.

• • •

"O Death the Healer"

AESCHYLUS

O Death the Healer, scorn thou not, I pray,
To come to me: of cureless ills thou art
The one physician. Pain lays not its touch
Upon a corpse.

Translated from the Greek by E.H. Plumptre

• • •

From "Mortality"

WILLIAM KNOX

O why should the spirit of mortal be proud?
Like a fast-flitting meteor, a fast-flying cloud,
A flash of the lightning, a break of the wave,
He passes from life to his rest in the grave.

The leaves of the oak and the willow shall fade,
Be scattered around, and together be laid;
And the young and the old, and the low and the high,
Shall moulder to dust, and together shall lie.

The child that a mother attended and loved,
The mother that infant's affection that proved;
The husband that mother and infant that blessed,
Each, all, are away to their dwelling of rest.

The maid on whose cheek, on whose brow, in whose eye,
Shone beauty and pleasure,—her triumphs are by;
And the memory of those that beloved her and praised
Are alike from the minds of the living erased.

The hand of the king that the scepter hath borne,
The brow of the priest that the miter hath worn,
The eye of the sage, and the heart of the brave,
Are hidden and lost in the depths of the grave.

The peasant whose lot was to sow and to reap,
The herdsman who climbed with his goats to the steep,
The beggar that wandered in search of his bread,
Have faded away like the grass that we tread.

The saint that enjoyed the communion of heaven,
The sinner that dared to remain unforgiven,
The wise and the foolish, the guilty and just,
Have quietly mingled their bones in the dust.

So the multitude goes, like the flower and the weed
That wither away to let others succeed;
So the multitude comes, even those we behold,
To repeat every tale that hath often been told.

• • •

"A Very Ancient Ode" (from *Japanese Literature*)

ANONYMOUS

Mountains and ocean-waves
Around me lie;
Forever the mountain-chains
Tower to the sky;
Fixed is the ocean
Immutably:—
Man is a thing of nought,
Born but to die!

Translated from the Japanese by Epiphanius Wilson

• • •

From "Thanatopsis"

WILLIAM CULLEN BRYANT

Yet a few days, and thee
The all-beholding sun shall see no more
In all his course; nor yet in the cold ground,
Where thy pale form was laid, with many tears,
Nor in the embrace of ocean, shall exist
Thy image. Earth, that nourished thee, shall claim
Thy growth, to be resolved to earth again,
And, lost each human trace, surrendering up
Thine individual being, shalt thou go
To mix for ever with the elements,
To be a brother to the insensible rock

And to the sluggish clod, which the rude swain
Turns with his share, and treads upon. The oak
Shall send his roots abroad, and pierce thy mould.
    Yet not to thine eternal resting-place
Shalt thou retire alone, nor couldst thou wish
Couch more magnificent. Thou shalt lie down
With patriarchs of the infant world—with kings,
The powerful of the earth—the wise, the good,
Fair forms, and hoary seers of ages past,
All in one mighty sepulchre. The hills
Rock-ribbed and ancient as the sun,—the vales
Stretching in pensive quietness between;
The venerable woods—rivers that move
In majesty, and the complaining brooks
That make the meadows green; and, poured round all,
Old Ocean's gray and melancholy waste,—
Are but the solemn decorations all
Of the great tomb of man.

· · ·

From "Sunday Morning"

WALLACE STEVENS

Death is the mother of beauty; hence from her,
Alone, shall come fulfilment to our dreams
And our desires. Although she strews the leaves
Of sure obliteration on our paths,
The path sick sorrow took, the many paths
Where triumph rang its brassy phrase, or love
Whispered a little out of tenderness,
She makes the willow shiver in the sun
For maidens who were wont to sit and gaze
Upon the grass, relinquished to their feet.
She causes boys to pile new plums and pears
On disregarded plate. The maidens taste
And stray impassioned in the littering leaves.

VI

Is there no change of death in paradise?
Does ripe fruit never fall? Or do the boughs
Hang always heavy in that perfect sky,
Unchanging, yet so like our perishing earth,
With rivers like our own that seek for seas
They never find, the same receding shores
That never touch with inarticulate pang?
Why set the pear upon those river banks
Or spice the shores with odors of the plum?
Alas, that they should wear our colors there,
The silken weavings of our afternoons,
And pick the strings of our insipid lutes!
Death is the mother of beauty, mystical,
Within whose burning bosom we devise
Our earthly mothers waiting, sleeplessly.

• • •

Death—Divination

CHARLES WHARTON STORK

Death is like moonlight in a lofty wood,
    That pours pale magic through the shadowy leaves;
    'T is like the web that some old perfume weaves
In a dim, lonely room where memories brood;
Like snow-chilled wine it steals into the blood,
    Spurring the pulse its coolness half reprieves;
    Tenderly quickening impulses it gives,
As April winds unsheathe an opening bud.

Death is like all sweet, sense-enfolding things,
    That lift us in a dream-delicious trance
    Beyond the flickering good and ill of chance;
But most is Death like Music's buoyant wings,
    That bear the soul, a willing Ganymede,
    Where joys on joys forevermore succeed.

• • •

From "Sîva" ["Shiva"]

SIR ALFRED COMYN LYALL

'Mors Janua Vitae.'

I am the God of the sensuous fire
    That moulds all Nature in forms divine;
The symbols of death and of man's desire,
    The springs of change in the world, are mine;
The organs of birth and the circlet of bones,
And the light loves carved on the temple stones.

I am the lord of delights and pain,
    Of the pest that killeth, of fruitful joys;
I rule the currents of heart and vein;
    A touch gives passion, a look destroys;
In the heat and cold of my lightest breath
Is the might incarnate of Lust and Death.

If a thousand altars stream with blood
    Of the victims slain by the chanting priest,
Is a great God lured by the savoury food?
    I reck not of worship, or song, or feast;
But that millions perish, each hour that flies,
Is the mystic sign of my sacrifice.

Ye may plead and pray for the millions born;
    They come like dew on the morning grass;
Your vows and vigils I hold in scorn,
    The soul stays never, the stages pass;
All life is the play of the power that stirs
In the dance of my wanton worshippers.

And the strong swift river my shrine below
    It runs, like man, its unending course
To the boundless sea from eternal snow;
    Mine is the Fountain—and mine the Force
That spurs all nature to ceaseless strife;
And my image is Death at the gates of Life.

19

In many a legend and many a shape,
    In the solemn grove and the crowded street,
I am the Slayer, whom none escape;
    I am Death trod under a fair girl's feet;
I govern the tides of the sentient sea
That ebbs and flows to eternity.

And the sum of the thought and the knowledge of man
    Is the secret tale that my emblems tell;
Do ye seek God's purpose, or trace his plan?
    Ye may read your doom in my parable:
For the circle of life in its flower and its fall
Is the writing that runs on my temple wall . . .

Let my temples fall, they are dark with age,
    Let my idols break, they have stood their day;
On their deep hewn stones the primeval sage
    Has figured the spells that endure alway;
My presence may vanish from river and grove,
But I rule for ever in Death and Love.

• • •

Dirge in Woods

GEORGE MEREDITH

A wind sways the pines,
    And below
Not a breath of wild air;
Still as the mosses that glow
On the flooring and over the lines
Of the roots here and there.
The pine-tree drops its dead;
They are quiet, as under the sea.
Overhead, overhead

Rushes life in a race,
As the clouds the clouds chase;
    And we go,
And we drop like the fruits of the tree,
      Even we,
      Even so.

• • •

"I like a look of agony"

EMILY DICKINSON

I like a look of agony,
Because I know it's true;
Men do not sham convulsion,
Nor simulate a throe.

The eyes glaze once, and that is death.
Impossible to feign
The beads upon the forehead
By homely anguish strung.

• • •

Birth and Death

THOMAS WADE

Methinks the soul within the body held
Is as a little babe within the womb,
Which flutters in its antenatal tomb,
But stirs and heaves the prison where 't is cell'd,
And struggles in strange darkness, undispell'd
By all its strivings towards the breath and bloom
Of that aurorean being soon to come—
Strivings of feebleness, by nothing quell'd:
And even as birth to the enfranchis'd child,

Which shows to its sweet senses all the vast
Of beauty visible and audible,
Is death unto the spirit undefil'd;
Setting it free of limit, and the past,
And all that in its prison-house befell.

· · ·

Anatomy

LINDA HOGAN

Inside the womb of the mother,
the spine is the first formed,
even before the heart begins
and all the pathways of the body soon
will lead there, the contents
of which you can never doubt,
the red rush of blood
as if we swim with fire
or it with us in a circular flood.

After birth, the navel remains
so you can never forget you weren't a first person,
but one humble from the past, soon
to disappear into the future.

We are noble gases and crude elements, carbon,
and through history have been wrapped in silk,
encased in gold,
embalmed with cloves, amber, pollen,
as we have also been torn to the bone
and treated as if not ever divine or vulnerable
by the rages and fears of others.

But what body part is it that dreams?
Not the lens of the eye, not the ear,
but an unknown part entranced,

the part that listens to gods,
speaks to mortals,
the one who, at the end,
when it all comes apart
and the soul leaves, not merely like at night
in a dream,
you think of the heart,
how love should be the last thing to disappear
with the history of a person's life bent by time,
or the ripening of bruised beauty.

Remember, then the first thing to form was the spine
but the last to disappear
is the sacrum, the tailbone,
as if the body remembers the fine animal
that was lost
some place in time.

· · ·

On a Grave in Christ-Church, Hants

OSCAR FAY ADAMS

Turning from Shelley's sculptured face aside,
And pacing thoughtfully the silent aisles
Of the gray church that overlooks the smiles
Of the glad Avon hastening its tide
To join the seaward-winding Stour, I spied
Close at my feet a slab among the tiles
That paved the minster, where the sculptor's files
Had graven only "Died of Grief," beside
The name of her who slept below. Sad soul!
A century has fled since kindly death
Cut short that life which nothing knew but grief,
And still your fate stirs pity. Yet the whole
Wide world is full of graves like yours, for breath
Of sorrow kills as oft as frost the leaf.

· · ·

A Ring

W.S. MERWIN

At this moment
this earth which for all we know

is the only place in the vault of darkness
with life on it is wound in a fine veil

of whispered voices groping the frayed waves
of absence they keep flaring up

out of hope entwined with its opposite
to wander in ignorance as we do

when we look for what we have lost
one moment touching the earth and the next

straying far out past the orbits and webs
and the static of knowledge they go on

without being able to tell whether
they are addressing the past or the future

or knowing there they are heard these words
of the living talking to the dead.

• • •

From *Paradise Lost*

JOHN MILTON

Death thou hast seen
In his first shape on Man; but many shapes
Of Death, and many are the ways that lead
To his grim cave, all dismal; yet to sense
More terrible at the entrance, than within.

• • •

"Ye hasten to the grave! What seek ye there"

PERCY BYSSHE SHELLEY

Ye hasten to the grave! What seek ye there,
Ye restless thoughts and busy purposes
Of the idle brain, which the world's livery wear?
O thou quick heart, which pantest to possess
All that pale Expectation feigneth fair!
Thou vainly curious mind, which wouldest guess
Whence thou didst come, and whither thou must go,
And all that never yet was known would know—
O whither hasten ye, that thus ye press
With such swift feet life's green and pleasant path,
Seeking, alike from happiness and woe,
A refuge in the cavern of grey death?
O heart, and mind, and thoughts! what thing do you
Hope to inherit in the grave below?

• • •

To His Watch When He Could Not Sleep

LORD HERBERT OF CHERBURY

Uncessant minutes, whilst you move you tell
The time that tells our life, which, though it run
Never so fast or far, your new-begun
Short steps shall overtake; for though life well

May 'scape his own account, it shall not yours;
You are Death's auditors, that both divide
And sum whate'er that life inspired endures
Past a beginning, and through you we bide

The doom of Fate, whose unrecalled decree
You date, bring, execute; making what's new
(Ill and good) old; for as we die in you,
You die in Time, Time in Eternity.

• • •

From *Ajax*

SOPHOCLES

The long march of the innumerable hours
Brings from the darkness all things to birth,
And all things born envelops in the night.

Translated from the Greek by Robert Whitelaw

• • •

Only Death

PABLO NERUDA

There are lone cemeteries,
tombs filled with soundless bones,
the heart passing through a tunnel
dark, dark, dark;
like a shipwreck we die inward,
like smothering in our hearts,
like slowly falling from our skin down to our soul.

There are corpses,
there are feet of sticky, cold gravestone,
there is death in the bones,
like a pure sound,
like a bark without a dog,
coming from certain bells, from certain tombs,
growing in the dampness like teardrops or raindrops.

I see alone, at times,
coffins with sails
weighing anchor with pale corpses, with dead-tressed women,
with bakers white as angels,
with pensive girls married to notaries,
coffins going up the vertical river of the dead,

the dark purple river,
upstream, with the sails swollen by the sound of death,
swollen by the silent sound of death.

To resonance comes death
like a shoe without a foot, like a suit without a man,
she comes to knock with a stoneless and fingerless ring,
she comes to shout without mouth, without tongue, without throat.
Yet her steps sound
and her dress sounds, silent, like a tree.

I know little, I am not well acquainted, I can scarcely see,
but I think that her song has the color of moist violets,
of violets accustomed to the earth,
because the face of death is green,
and the gaze of death is green,
with the sharp dampness of a violet leaf
and its dark color of exasperated winter.

But death also goes through the world dressed as a broom,
she licks the ground looking for corpses,
death is in the broom,
it is death's tongue looking for dead bodies,
it is death's needle looking for thread.

Death is in the cots:
in the slow mattresses, in the black blankets
she lives stretched out, and she suddenly blows:
she blows a dark sound that puffs out sheets,
and there are beds sailing to a port
where she is waiting, dressed as an admiral.

Translated from the Spanish by Donald D. Walsh

• • •

"Death only craves not gifts"

AESCHYLUS

Of all the gods, Death only craves not gifts:
Nor sacrifice, nor yet drink-offering poured
Avails; no altars hath he, nor is soothed
By hymns of praise. From him alone of all
The powers of heaven Persuasion holds aloof.

Translated from the Greek by E.H. Plumptre

• • •

The Dead

MATHILDE BLIND

The dead abide with us! Though stark and cold
   Earth seems to grip them, they are with us still:
   They have forged our chains of being for good or ill
And their invisible hands these hands yet hold.
Our perishable bodies are the mould
   In which their strong imperishable will—
   Mortality's deep yearning to fulfill—
Hath grown incorporate through dim time untold.

Vibrations infinite of life in death,
   As a star's travelling light survives its star!
   So may we hold our lives, that when we are
The fate of those who then will draw this breath,
   They shall not drag us to their judgment-bar
And curse the heritage which we bequeath.

• • •

The World Is a Hunt

WILLIAM DRUMMOND OF HAWTHORNDEN

The World a-hunting is:
The prey poor Man, the Nimrod fierce is Death;
His speedy greyhounds are
Lust, Sickness, Envy, Care,
Strife that ne'er falls amiss,
With all those ills which haunt us while we breathe.
Now if by chance we fly
Of these the eager chase,
Old Age with stealing pace
Casts up his nets, and there we panting die.

•   •   •

Homo Sapiens

JOHN WILMOT, EARL OF ROCHESTER

Were I (who to my cost already am
One of those strange, prodigious creatures, man)
A spirit free to choose, for my own share,
What case of flesh and blood I pleased to wear,
I'd be a dog, a monkey, or a bear,
Or anything but that vain animal
Who is so proud of being rational.
The senses are too gross, and he'll contrive
A sixth, to contradict the other five,
And before certain instinct, will prefer
Reason, which fifty times for one does err;
Reason, an *ignis fatuus* in the mind,
Which, leaving light of nature, sense, behind,
Pathless and dangerous wandering ways it takes
Through error's fenny bogs and thorny brakes;
Whilst the misguided follower climbs with pain
Mountains of whimseys, heaped in his own brain;

Stumbling from thought to thought, falls headlong down
Into doubt's boundless sea, where, like to drown,
Books bear him up awhile, and make him try
To swim with bladders of philosophy;
In hopes still to o'ertake the escaping light,
The vapour dances in his dazzling sight
Till, spent, it leaves him to eternal night.
Then old age and experience, hand in hand,
Lead him to death, and make him understand,
After a search so painful and so long,
That all his life he has been in the wrong.
Huddled in dirt the reasoning engine lies,
Who was so proud, so witty, and so wise.

• • •

The Old Man Who Made No Lamentation at the Death of His Sons (from *The Masnavi*)

RUMI

An old man who was noted for sanctity, and who realized the saying of the Prophet, "The 'ulama of the faith are as the prophets of Israel," lost all his sons, but showed no grief or regret. His wife therefore rebuked him for his want of feeling, whereupon he replied to her as follows:

He turned to his wife and said,
"The harvest of December is not as that of July;
Though they be dead or though they be living,
Are they not equally visible to the eyes of the heart?
I behold them clearly before me,
Wherefore should I disfigure my countenance like you?
Though they have gone forth by revolution of fortune,
They are with me still, playing round me.
The cause of lamentation is separation or parting,
But I am still with my dear ones, and embrace them.
Ordinary people may see them in dreams,
But I see them clearly, though wide awake.

I conceal myself a while from this world,
I shake down the leaves of outward sense from the tree.
Know, O wife, outward sense is captive to reason,
And reason, again, is captive to spirit.
Spirit unlooses the chained hands of reason;
Yea, it opens all things that are closed.
Sensations and thoughts resemble weeds
Which occupy the surface of pure water.
The hand of reason puts these weeds aside,
And the pure water is then visible to the wise.
Weeds in plenty cover the stream like bubbles;
When they are swept aside, the water is seen;
But when God unlooses not the hands of reason,
The weeds on our water grow thick through carnal lust;
Yea, they cover up your water more and more,
While your lust is smiling and your reason weeping.
When fear of God binds the hands of lust,
Then God unlooses the two hands of reason.
Then the powerful senses are subdued by you,
When you submit to reason as your commander
Then your sleepless sense is lulled into sleep,
That mysteries may appear to the soul.
You behold visions when broad awake,
And the gates of heaven are open before you."

Translated from the Persian by E.H. Whinfield

•　•　•

31

"If I should die"

EMILY DICKINSON

If I should die,
And you should live,
And time should gurgle on,
And morn should beam,
And noon should burn,
As it has usual done;
If birds should build as early,
And bees as bustling go,—
One might depart at option
From enterprise below!
'T is sweet to know that stocks will stand
When we with daisies lie,
That commerce will continue,
And trades as briskly fly.
It makes the parting tranquil
And keeps the soul serene,
That gentlemen so sprightly
Conduct the pleasing scene!

. . .

From *Night Thoughts*

EDWARD YOUNG

The dread of death! I sing its sovereign cure.
Why start at Death? Where is he? Death arrived,
Is past; not come, or gone, he's never here.
Ere hope, sensation fails; black-boding man
Receives, not suffers, Death's tremendous blow.
The knell, the shroud, the mattock, and the grave;
The deep damp vault, the darkness, and the worm;
These are the bugbears of a winter's eve,
The terrors of the living, not the dead.
Imagination's fool, and error's wretch,

Man makes a death, which nature never made;
Then on the point of his own fancy falls;
And feels a thousand deaths, in fearing one.

.   .   .

The Voice

SARA TEASDALE

Atoms as old as stars,
Mutation on mutation,
Millions and millions of cells
Dividing yet still the same,
From air and changing earth,
From ancient Eastern rivers,
From turquoise tropic seas,
Unto myself I came.

My spirit like my flesh
Sprang from a thousand sources,
From cave-man, hunter and shepherd,
From Karnak, Cyprus, Rome;
The living thoughts in me
Spring from dead men and women,
Forgotten time out of mind
And many as bubbles of foam.

Here for a moment's space
Into the light out of darkness,
I come and they come with me
Finding words with my breath;
From the wisdom of many life-times
I hear them cry: "Forever
Seek for Beauty, she only
Fights with man against Death!"

.   .   .

On the World

FRANCIS QUARLES

The world's an Inn; and I her guest.
I eat; I drink; I take my rest.
My hostess, nature, does deny me
Nothing, wherewith she can supply me;
Where, having stayed a while, I pay
Her lavish bills, and go my way.

. . .

All Things Decay and Die

ROBERT HERRICK

All things decay with time: the forest sees
The growth and downfall of her aged trees;
That timber tall, which threescore lusters stood
The proud dictator of the state-like wood,
I mean (the sovereign of all plants) the oak,
Droops, dies, and falls without the cleaver's stroke.

. . .

Hamlet's soliloquy

WILLIAM SHAKESPEARE

To be, or not to be: that is the question:
Whether 'tis nobler in the mind to suffer
The slings and arrows of outrageous fortune,
Or to take arms against a sea of troubles,
And by opposing end them? To die: to sleep;
No more; and by a sleep to say we end
The heart-ache and the thousand natural shocks
That flesh is heir to, 'tis a consummation
Devoutly to be wish'd. To die, to sleep;

To sleep: perchance to dream: ay, there's the rub;
For in that sleep of death what dreams may come
When we have shuffled off this mortal coil,
Must give us pause: there's the respect
That makes calamity of so long life;
For who would bear the whips and scorns of time,
The oppressor's wrong, the proud man's contumely,
The pangs of despised love, the law's delay,
The insolence of office and the spurns
That patient merit of the unworthy takes,
When he himself might his quietus make
With a bare bodkin? who would fardels bear,
To grunt and sweat under a weary life,
But that the dread of something after death,
The undiscover'd country from whose bourn
No traveller returns, puzzles the will
And makes us rather bear those ills we have
Than fly to others that we know not of?

•   •   •

The Death of the Poor

CHARLES BAUDELAIRE

It's Death that comforts us, alas! and makes us live;
It is the goal of life; it is the only hope
Which, like an elixir, makes us inebriate
And gives us the courage to march until evening;

Through the storm and the snow and the hoar-frost
It is the vibrant light on our black horizon;
It is the famous inn inscribed upon the book,
Where one can eat, and sleep, and take his rest;

It's an Angel who holds in his magnetic hands
Sleep and the gift of ecstatic dreams
And who makes the beds for the poor, naked people;

It's the glory of the gods, the mystic granary,
It is the poor man's purse, his ancient fatherland,
It is the portal opening on unknown Skies!

Translated from the French by William Aggeler

•   •   •

From *The Bhagavad Gita*

Arjuna:
How can I, in the battle, shoot with shafts
On Bhishma, or on Drona—O thou Chief!—
Both worshipful, both honourable men?
Better to live on beggar's bread
With those we love alive,
Than taste their blood in rich feasts spread,
And guiltily survive!
Ah! were it worse—who knows?—to be
Victor or vanquished here,
When those confront us angrily
Whose death leaves living drear?
In pity lost, by doubtings tossed,
My thoughts—distracted—turn
To Thee, the Guide I reverence most,
That I may counsel learn:
I know not what would heal the grief
Burned into soul and sense,
If I were earth's unchallenged chief—
A god—and these gone thence!

Krishna:
Thou grievest where no grief should be! thou speak'st
Words lacking wisdom! for the wise in heart
Mourn not for those that live, nor those that die.
Nor I, nor thou, nor any one of these,

Ever was not, nor ever will not be,
For ever and for ever afterwards.
All, that doth live, lives always! To man's frame
As there come infancy and youth and age,
So come there raisings-up and layings-down
Of other and of other life-abodes,
Which the wise know, and fear not. This that irks—
Thy sense-life, thrilling to the elements—
Bringing thee heat and cold, sorrows and joys,
'Tis brief and mutable! Bear with it, Prince!
As the wise bear. The soul which is not moved,
The soul that with a strong and constant calm
Takes sorrow and takes joy indifferently,
Lives in the life undying! That which is
Can never cease to be; that which is not
Will not exist. To see this truth of both
Is theirs who part essence from accident,
Substance from shadow. Indestructible,
Learn thou! the Life is, spreading life through all;
It cannot anywhere, by any means,
Be anywise diminished, stayed, or changed.
But for these fleeting frames which it informs
With spirit deathless, endless, infinite,
They perish. Let them perish, Prince! and fight!
He who shall say, "Lo! I have slain a man!"
He who shall think, "Lo! I am slain!" those both
Know naught! Life cannot slay. Life is not slain!
Never the spirit was born; the spirit shall cease to be never;
Never was time it was not; End and Beginning are dreams!
Birthless and deathless and changeless remaineth the spirit for ever;
Death hath not touched it at all, dead though the house of it seems!

Translated from the Sanskrit by Edwin Arnold

• • •

The Suicide's Argument

SAMUEL TAYLOR COLERIDGE

Ere the birth of my life, if I wished it or no
No question was asked me—it could not be so!
If the life was the question, a thing sent to try
And to live on be Yes; what can No be? to die.

NATURE'S ANSWER
Is't returned, as 'twas sent? Is't no worse for the wear?
Think first, what you are! Call to mind what you were!
I gave you innocence, I gave you hope,
Gave health, and genius, and an ample scope,
Return you me guilt, lethargy, despair?
Make out the invent'ry; inspect, compare!
Then die—if die you dare!

• • •

From "The Suicide"

ROBERT BLAIR

   Our time is fix'd, and all our days are number'd!
How long, how short, we know not: this we know,
Duty requires we calmly wait the summons,
Nor dare to stir till Heaven shall give permission:
Like sentries that must keep their destin'd stand,
And wait th' appointed hour till they're reliev'd.
Those only are the brave that keep their ground,
And keep it to the last. To run away
Is but a coward's trick: to run away
From this world's ills, that at the very worst
Will soon blow o'er, thinking to mend ourselves
By boldly venturing on a world unknown,
And plunging headlong in the dark 'tis mad!
No frenzy half so desperate as this.

• • •

Call

LINDA HOGAN

I don't know what you call it
when the lion sounds wounded and calls
the smaller animals
with their healthy coats and paws,
and they go as if death knows their language
and can change it to another.
The wolf, too, knows the words of elk and moose
and how to call them forward
and with the coyote the lovely vole arises
with soft fur from underground.
This, this is how some hear their god
and wander off toward it or him
and then are taken in
while the god walks on mighty and full,
passing others, generous at last.

• • •

From *An Essay on Man*

Alexander Pope

    Look round our world; behold the Chain of Love
Combining all below and all above.
See plastic nature working to this end,
The single atoms each to other tend,
Attract, attracted to, the next in place
Form'd and impell'd its neighbour to embrace.
See matter next, with various life endu'd,
Press to one centre still, the gen'ral good.
See dying vegetables life sustain,
See life dissolving vegetate again:
All forms that perish other forms supply,
(By turns we catch the vital breath, and die),
Like bubbles on the sea of matter born,

They rise, they break, and to that sea return.
Nothing is foreign; parts relate to whole;
One all-extending, all-preserving soul
Connects each being, greatest with the least;
Made beast in aid of man, and man of beast;
All serv'd, all serving: nothing stands alone;
The chain holds on, and where it ends, unknown.

．　．　．

Small

KATERINA STOYKOVA-KLEMER

Like the clasp of a necklace
death is a fairly small
part of life.

seeing death

In which the poets encounter Death in the flesh

My Number

BILLY COLLINS

Is Death miles away from this house,
reaching for a widow in Cincinnati
or breathing down the neck of a lost hiker
in British Columbia?

Is he too busy making arrangements,
tampering with air brakes,
scattering cancer cells like seeds,
loosening the wooden beams of roller coasters

to bother with my hidden cottage
that visitors find so hard to find?

Or is he stepping from a black car
parked at the dark end of the lane,
shaking open the familiar cloak,
its hood raised like the head of a crow,
and removing the scythe from the trunk?

Did you have any trouble with the directions?
I will ask, as I start talking my way out of this.

• • •

"Because I could not stop for Death"

EMILY DICKINSON

Because I could not stop for Death,
He kindly stopped for me;
The carriage held but just ourselves
And Immortality.

We slowly drove, he knew no haste,
And I had put away
My labor, and my leisure too,
For his civility.

We passed the school where children played
At wrestling in a ring;
We passed the fields of gazing grain,
We passed the setting sun.

We paused before a house that seemed
A swelling of the ground;
The roof was scarcely visible,
The cornice but a mound.

Since then 'tis centuries; but each
Feels shorter than the day
I first surmised the horses' heads
Were toward eternity.

• • •

Ballad for a Goth Chick

JENNIFER PERRINE

When Mary first saw Death, he had one arm
slung over her best friend's shoulder.
Mary could see how Susan had fallen
for someone like Death, the older

man, confident and debonair, who left
teenage Susan gasping for breath
the way none of her gangly classmates could.
She was captivated by Death,

and when he finally left her, Susan
never quite returned to normal.
Mary scarcely cared—she flirted with Death,
though he wasn't into formal

relationships. Death was sexy, he could
have any woman he wanted—
or man, for that matter—so Mary dressed
for Death. Her short black sheath flaunted

the legs she wrapped in tall boots and fishnets
that whispered and sighed as she walked.
She wanted Death to notice, willed his eyes
to follow her the way hers stalked

him. Sometimes Death filled Mary's thoughts, and when
she lay in bed, night dragging dark
skirts across the sky, she imagined him
shifting against her sheets, the arc

of his back pale as the moonlit surface
of the lake where she sometimes played
at suicide, wading in until her
head vanished. It was Death that made

her writhe up for air—after all, what if
Death came for her, what if today
Mary would lean into his kiss at last,
Death bending to meet her halfway?

• • •

From "When Lilacs Last in the Dooryard Bloom'd"

WALT WHITMAN

Come lovely and soothing death,
Undulate round the world, serenely arriving, arriving,
In the day, in the night, to all, to each,
Sooner or later delicate death.

Prais'd be the fathomless universe,
For life and joy, and for objects and knowledge curious,
And for love, sweet love—but praise! praise! praise!
For the sure-enwinding arms of cool-enfolding death.

Dark mother always gliding near with soft feet,
Have none chanted for thee a chant of fullest welcome?
Then I chant it for thee, I glorify thee above all,
I bring thee a song that when thou must indeed come, come unfalteringly.

Approach strong deliveress,
When it is so, when thou hast taken them I joyously sing the dead,
Lost in the loving floating ocean of thee,
Laved in the flood of thy bliss O death.

From me to thee glad serenades,
Dances for thee I propose saluting thee, adornments and feastings for thee,
And the sights of the open landscape and the high-spread sky are fitting,
And life and the fields, and the huge and thoughtful night.

The night in silence under many a star,
The ocean shore and the husky whispering wave whose voice I know,
And the soul turning to thee O vast and well-veil'd death,
And the body gratefully nestling close to thee.

Over the tree-tops I float thee a song,
Over the rising and sinking waves, over the myriad fields and the prairies
 wide,
Over the dense-pack'd cities all and the teeming wharves and ways,
I float this carol with joy, with joy to thee O death.

•   •   •

"Death, be not proud" (from *Holy Sonnets*)

JOHN DONNE

Death, be not proud, though some have called thee
Mighty and dreadful, for thou are not so;
For those whom thou think'st thou dost overthrow
Die not, poor Death, nor yet canst thou kill me.
From rest and sleep, which but thy pictures be,
Much pleasure; then from thee much more must flow,
And soonest our best men with thee do go,
Rest of their bones, and soul's delivery.
Thou art slave to fate, chance, kings, and desperate men,
And dost with poison, war, and sickness dwell,
And poppy or charms can make us sleep as well
And better than thy stroke; why swell'st thou then?
One short sleep past, we wake eternally,
And death shall be no more; Death, thou shalt die.

•   •   •

Newborn Death

DANTE GABRIEL ROSSETTI

To-day Death seems to me an infant child
Which her worn mother Life upon my knee
Has set to grow my friend and play with me;
If haply so my heart might be beguil'd
To find no terrors in a face so mild,—

If haply so my weary heart might be
Unto the newborn milky eyes of thee,
O Death, before resentment reconcil'd.
How long, O Death? And shall thy feet depart
Still a young child's with mine, or wilt thou stand
Fullgrown the helpful daughter of my heart,
What time with thee indeed I reach the strand
Of the pale wave which knows thee what thou art,
And drink it in the hollow of thy hand?

• • •

Spring and Death

GERARD MANLEY HOPKINS

I had a dream. A wondrous thing:
It seem'd an evening in the Spring:
—A little sickness in the air
From too much fragrance everywhere:—
As I walk'd a stilly wood,
Sudden, Death before me stood:
In a hollow lush and damp,
He seem'd a dismal mirky stamp
On the flowers that were seen
His charnelhouse-grate rips between,
And with his coffin-black he barr'd the green.
"Death," said I, "what do you here
At this Spring season of the year?"
"I mark the flowers ere the prime
Which I may tell at Autumn-time."
Ere I had further question made
Death was vanish'd from the glade.
Then I saw that he had bound
Many trees and flowers round
With a subtle web of black,
And that such a sable track
Lay along the grasses green

From the spot where he had been.
But the Spring-tide pass'd the same;
Summer was as full of flame;
Autumn-time no earlier came.
And the flowers that he had tied,
As I mark'd not always died
Sooner than their mates; and yet
Their fall was fuller of regret:
It seem'd so hard and dismal thing,
Death, to mark them in the Spring.

. . .

The Junk Man

CARL SANDBURG

I am glad God saw Death
And gave Death a job taking care of all who are tired of living:

When all the wheels in a clock are worn and slow and the connections
loose
And the clock goes on ticking and telling the wrong time from hour to
hour
And people around the house joke about what a bum clock it is,
How glad the clock is when the big Junk Man drives his wagon
Up to the house and puts his arms around the clock and says:
"You don't belong here,
You gotta come
Along with me,"
How glad the clock is then, when it feels the arms of the Junk Man close
around it and carry it away.

. . .

Question

LANGSTON HUGHES

When the old junk man Death
Comes to gather up our bodies
And toss them into the sack of oblivion,
I wonder if he will find
The corpse of a white multi-millionaire
Worth more pennies of eternity,
Than the black torso of
A Negro cotton-picker?

· · ·

Epitaph

E.E. CUMMINGS

Tumbling-hair
           picker of buttercups
                        violets
dandelions
And the big bullying daisies
                    through the field wonderful
with eyes a little sorry
Another comes
        also picking flowers

· · ·

Babies

STANLEY MOSS

Babies, babies,
before you can see more than light or darkness,
before your mothers have kissed your heads,
I come to you with news of dead and dying friends.
You so close to the miracle of life,
lend me a miracle to bring to my friend.
Babies, babies.
Once Death was a baby, he grasped God's little finger
to keep from falling—kicking and chortling
on his back, unbaptised, uncircumcised,
but invited to share sunlight and darkness
with the rest of us. Mother Death would nurse him,
comfort and wash him when he soiled himself
in the arms of the mourners and heartbroken.

Older, Death took his place
at table beside his mother—her "angel."
They ate and drank from each other's mouths and fingers,
laughed at their private jokes. He could play
any musical instrument, knew all music by heart,
all birdsong, the purr, growl, snort, or whine
of each and every animal.
The story goes that, fat with eternal life,
older than his mother, he devoured her,
far from light or darkness.

Babies, at the moment of your first uncertain breath,
when your mother's magic blood is still upon you,
I come to you, the helpless ones still coughing
from miracles of birth.
Babies hardly heavier than clouds,
in desperation, for my friend, for a lark
I hold up the sac you broke through
as if it were Saint Veronica's Veil—
but no face is on it, no blood.

I hold up a heavy sack of useless words.
I shake a rattle to catch your first eye or smile.

. . .

Death's Epitaph

PHILIP FRENEAU

Death in this tomb his weary bones hath laid,
Sick of dominion o'er the human kind—
Behold what devastation he hath made,
Survey the millions by his arm confined.

Six thousand years has sovereign sway been
None, but myself, can real glory claim;
Great Regent of the world I reigned alone,
And princes trembled when my mandate came.

Vast and unmatched throughout the world my fame
Takes place of gods, and asks no mortal date—
No; by myself, and by the heavens, I swear,
Not Alexander's name is half so great.

Nor swords nor darts my prowess could withstand,
All quit their arms, and bowed to my decree,
Even mighty Julius died beneath my hand,
For slaves and C'sars were the same to me!

Traveller, would'st thou his noblest trophies seek,
Search in no narrow spot obscure for those;
The sea profound, the surface of all land,
Is moulded with the myriads of his foes.

. . .

To Death

CAROLINE BOWLES SOUTHEY

Come not in terrors clad, to claim
   An unresisting prey;
Come like an evening shadow, Death!
   So stealthily, so silently!
And shut mine eyes, and steal my breath;
   Then willingly—oh! willingly
  With thee I'll go away.

What need to clutch with iron grasp
   What gentlest touch may take?
What need, with aspect dark, to scare,
   So awfully, so terribly,
The weary soul would hardly care,
   Called quietly, called tenderly,
  From thy dread power to break?

'Tis not as when thou markest out
   The young, the blest, the gay,
The loved, the loving—they who dream
   So happily, so hopefully;
Then harsh thy kindest call may seem,
   And shrinkingly, reluctantly,
  The summoned may obey.

But I have drunk enough of life—
   The cup assigned to me
Dashed with a little sweet at best,
   So scantily, so scantily—
To know full well that all the rest,
   More bitterly, more bitterly,
  Drugged to the last will be.

And I may live to pain some heart
   That kindly cares for me—
To pain, but not to bless. O Death!
   Come quietly—come lovingly,
And shut mine eyes, and steal my breath;
   Then willingly—oh! willingly,
  With thee I'll go away.

        • • •

Madrigal

WILLIAM DRUMMOND OF HAWTHORNDEN

  My thoughts hold mortal strife;
  I do detest my life,
  And with lamenting cries
  Peace to my soul to bring
Oft call that prince which here doth monarchize:
   But he, grim-grinning King,
Who caitiffs scorns, and doth the blest surprise,
Late having deckt with beauty's rose his tomb,
Disdains to crop a weed, and will not come.

        • • •

Death Stands Above Me

WALTER SAVAGE LANDOR

Death stands above me, whispering low
I know not what into my ear;
Of his strange language all I know
Is, there is not a word of fear.

        • • •

Small Hours Poem

Lenore Kandel

I dream of death as sparrows dream of hawks
a presence up above and just beyond the eye
    a darkness in the sky

old bone man sits within my own sweet flesh
waiting me out with cool white patience

there are times he entices me
in the narrow part of the night, when I begin to lose faith in morning
and I am all and entirely alone

yet somehow night always ends in time and he lets go
he has the patience of an owner
as he slips inside
and loans me back my own white bones again
this contract is one-sided, old man!

he winks and sits inside
I shrug my borrowed bones and laugh at both of us

the morning smells so sweet . . .

• • •

The Grammarian

Stanley Moss

I say, to be silly,
Death is a grammarian.
He needs the simple past,
the *passato remoto*, the *passé composé*,
the *le* in Chinese added
to any verb in the present
that makes it past.

In the pluperfect houses of worship
death hangs around,
is thought to be undone.
Sometimes he is welcome.
I thank him for the simple present
and his patience.

those who have gone (and the ones still here)

In which the poets grieve, remember, and say goodbye
(occasionally the dead have their say, too)

Dirge Without Music

EDNA ST. VINCENT MILLAY

I am not resigned to the shutting away of loving hearts in the hard ground.
So it is, and so it will be, for so it has been, time out of mind:
Into the darkness they go, the wise and the lovely. Crowned
With lilies and with laurel they go; but I am not resigned.

Lovers and thinkers, into the earth with you.
Be one with the dull, the indiscriminate dust.
A fragment of what you felt, of what you knew,
A formula, a phrase remains,—but the best is lost.

The answers quick and keen, the honest look, the laughter, the love,—
They are gone. They are gone to feed the roses. Elegant and curled
Is the blossom. Fragrant is the blossom. I know. But I do not approve.
More precious was the light in your eyes than all the roses in the world.

Down, down, down into the darkness of the grave
Gently they go, the beautiful, the tender, the kind;
Quietly they go, the intelligent, the witty, the brave.
I know. But I do not approve. And I am not resigned.

• • •

"My life closed twice before its close"

EMILY DICKINSON

My life closed twice before its close;
   It yet remains to see
If Immortality unveil
   A third event to me,
So huge, so hopeless to conceive,
   As these that twice befell.
Parting is all we know of heaven,
   And all we need of hell.

• • •

The Departed

JOHN BANISTER TABB

They cannot wholly pass away,
    How far soe'er above;
Nor we, the lingerers, wholly stay
    Apart from those we love:
For spirits in eternity,
    As shadows in the sun,
Reach backward into Time, as we,
    Like lifted clouds, reach on.

• • •

Naming

CAROL LYNNE KNIGHT

If I name this grief,
define it
with guilt
and redemption,
call it drowning,
desolation,
call it
fire and stone,

then I am bound
to care for it,
like a stray cat I name,
that demands I feed him.
He comes and goes,
sometimes disappears
for days and then returns,
insisting that
I remember.

• • •

Silence

D.H. LAWRENCE

Since I lost you I am silence-haunted,
  Sounds wave their little wings
A moment, then in weariness settle
  On the flood that soundless swings.

Whether the people in the street
  Like pattering ripples go by,
Or whether the theatre sighs and sighs
  With a loud, hoarse sigh:

Or the wind shakes a ravel of light
  Over the dead-black river,
Or night's last echoing
  Makes the daybreak shiver:

I feel the silence waiting
  To take them all up again
In its vast completeness, enfolding
  The sound of men.

• • •

"The distance that the dead have gone"

EMILY DICKINSON

The distance that the dead have gone
Does not at first appear;
Their coming back seems possible
For many an ardent year.

And then, that we have followed them
We more than half suspect,
So intimate have we become
With their dear retrospect.

• • •

Stillbirth

LAURE-ANNE BOSSELAAR

On a platform, I heard someone call out your name:
No, Laetitia, no.
It wasn't my train—the doors were closing,
but I rushed in, searching for your face.

But no Laetitia. No.
No one in that car could have been you,
but I rushed in, searching for your face:
no longer an infant. A woman now, blond, thirty-two.

No one in that car could have been you.
Laetitia-Marie was the name I had chosen.
No longer an infant. A woman now, blond, thirty-two:
I sometimes go months without remembering you.

Laetitia-Marie was the name I had chosen:
I was told not to look. Not to get attached—
I sometimes go months without remembering you.
Some griefs bless us that way, not asking much space.

I was told not to look. Not to get attached.
It wasn't my train—the doors were closing.
Some griefs bless us that way, not asking much space.
On a platform, I heard someone calling your name.

• • •

the lost baby poem

LUCILLE CLIFTON

the time i dropped your almost body down
down to meet the waters under the city
and run one with the sewage to the sea
what did i know about waters rushing back
what did i know about drowning
or being drowned

you would have been born into winter
in the year of the disconnected gas
and no car   we would have made the thin
walk over genesee hill into the canada wind
to watch you slip like ice into strangers' hands
you would have fallen naked as snow into winter
if you were here i could tell you these
and some other things

if i am ever less than a mountain
for your definite brothers and sisters
let the rivers pour over my head
let the sea take me for a spiller
of seas   let black men call me stranger
always   for your never named sake

• • •

On the Death of My Son Charles

DANIEL WEBSTER

My son, thou wast my heart's delight,
  Thy morn of life was gay and cheery;
That morn has rushed to sudden night,
  Thy father's house is sad and dreary.

I held thee on my knee, my son!
  And kissed thee laughing, kissed thee weeping;
But ah! thy little day is done,
  Thou 'rt with thy angel sister sleeping.

The staff, on which my years should lean,
  Is broken, ere those years come o'er me;
My funeral rites thou shouldst have seen,
  But thou art in the tomb before me.

Thou rear'st to me no filial stone,
  No parent's grave with tears beholdest;
Thou art my ancestor, my son!
  And stand'st in Heaven's account the oldest.

On earth my lot was soonest cast,
  Thy generation after mine,
Thou hast thy predecessor past;
  Earlier eternity is thine.

I should have set before thine eyes
  The road to Heaven, and showed it clear;
But thou untaught spring'st to the skies,
  And leav'st thy teacher lingering here.

Sweet Seraph, I would learn of thee,
  And hasten to partake thy bliss!
And oh! to thy world welcome me,
  As first I welcomed thee to this.

Dear Angel, thou art safe in heaven;
  No prayers for thee need more be made;
Oh! let thy prayers for those be given
  Who oft have blessed thy infant head.

My father! I beheld thee born,
  And led thy tottering steps with care;
Before me risen to Heaven's bright morn,
  My son! my father! guide me there.

· · ·

On My First Daughter

BEN JONSON

Here lies, to each her parents' ruth,
Mary, the daughter of their youth;
Yet all heaven's gifts being heaven's due,
It makes the father less to rue.
At six months' end she parted hence
With safety of her innocence;
Whose soul heaven's queen, whose name she bears,
In comfort of her mother's tears,
Hath placed amongst her virgin-train:
Where, while that severed doth remain,
This grave partakes the fleshly birth;
Which cover lightly, gentle earth!

. . .

Ode to History

MARY JO BANG

Had she not lain on that bed with a boy
All those years ago, where would they be, she wondered.
She and the child that wouldn't have been but was now
No more. She would know nothing
Of mothering. She would know nothing
Of death. She would know nothing
Of love. The three things she'd been given
To remember. Wake me up, please, she said,
When this life is over. Look at her—It's as if
The windows of night have been sewn to her eyes.

. . .

Epitaph on the Lady Mary Villiers

THOMAS CAREW

The Lady Mary Villiers lies
Under this stone; with weeping eyes
The parents that first gave her birth,
And their sad friends, laid her in earth.
If any of them, Reader, were
Known unto thee, shed a tear;
Or if thyself possess a gem
As dear to thee, as this to them,
Though a stranger to this place,
Bewail in theirs thine own hard case:
    For thou perhaps at thy return
    May'st find thy Darling in an urn.

• • •

Mother's Lament

EMILY FERRARA

Your feet tagged,
tinged blue, hang
over the gurney's edge.
Head thrust back,
mouth slack,
hands folded cold
turning colder.
I reach for life
in your muscled body,
carefully sheathed.
Your cropped hair still
grows warm. I murmur,
touch your head, place
my mouth to your cheek.
Wrench free the taut sheet.

See your penis at rest:
crimson, pure, your blood rushed
all your lean pubescence to ripen there.
I want to cast out the affront
of the yellow catheter
still inserted in you.
All I want is your flesh,
slick and warm as the day
you were born.

• • •

How to Find Out

KATHLEEN SHEEDER BONANNO

◆

After you call her
again and again
on her home phone,
and your intention,
like a mouse in a snake's belly,
swells the wire
as it runs from one pole
to another
and still she doesn't answer—

after you call her
on her cell phone
and summon a satellite network
to assist,
to bounce your voice
from your house
to a floating point in space,
to her house,
and still she doesn't answer—
after you leave many messages,

and your husband leaves messages,
and your sister leaves messages,
and anxiety flits over and around you—

ignore it. She is an adult now.
Wait a day.

♦

First leave a final message:
We are going to drive
up there right now, young lady,
if you don't call us back in fifteen minutes.

And then start driving
in a hard rain,
you and Dave,
and when you get to Skippack
your cell phone will ring
and someone will say
she was just spotted
working her nursing shift
on the hospital floor.

Laugh and turn the car around then—
a ton of relief
barreling back down Route 73.

When you get home,
call the hospital,
just to make sure.

♦

Her supervisor will say
No, no, she's not here;
she hasn't shown up for work
in two days.

This is the time
for your throat to thicken,
for your fingers to get rubbery,
for you to call the police

and say, *Please please
go to her apartment and
if it's locked, please
knock down the door.*

♦

Now you and your husband
and sister and her husband
must jump into his car
and drive so fast you might crash;

hold your husband's hand hard
but do not look at him,
do not look him in the eyes
until one of you says,

Jesus, I have to go to the bathroom,
and all four of you run
into a diner somewhere
and as the patrons look up,
charge into the restroom
and pee hard,

so you don't wet your clothes later,
and take a moment
to dry heave a little into the toilet,
but not too much, there's no time.
♦

Pull up onto her street.
Jump out of the moving car
as your brother-in-law parks it.

Run past police cars,
ambulance,
all the silent people
sitting on curbs,
gathered on porches,
their arms folded
waiting for you,
the parents,
to arrive.

The chief of police,
poised behind the yellow tape,
will spread his long arms to you,
his palms outward.
This is it:
your very own
annunciation.

Try to be thoughtful,
don't make the poor man say it;
see how human he is,
he has children of his own,
it is your job to ask:
Is she dead?

And he will nod and say *yes.*
And now he can never not nod.
And now he can never say no.
And now he can never not say
yes.

• • •

Prayer Requests at a Mennonite Church

TODD DAVIS

Pray for the Smucker family. Their son Nathaniel's coat and shirt were caught in the gears while grinding grain. Nothing would give, so now he is gone. We made his clothes too well. Perhaps this is our sin.

Pray for the Birky family. Their son Jacob fell to his death in the granary. He was covered in corn before they could stop the pouring—chest crushed by the weight, seed spilling from his mouth. We hope something will grow from this, besides our grief.

Pray for the Hartzler family. Their youngest has left the church and no longer believes that Christ died for her sins. She buys clothes at the mall. Tongue pierced, nose as well. Her shirt shows her belly where a ring of gold sprouts. We pray she will remember that her Lord's side was pierced, that His crown held no gold, only the dried blood of His brow.

Pray for the Miller family. Last week their daughter, who lives in Kalona, lost her baby at birth. Child only half-formed: head turned the wrong way; heart laid on the outside of her chest; one leg little more than an afterthought. Lord, help them know that life may come again, that we are all made whole in heaven.

Pray for the Stutzman family. Their son fights in the war. We call him back to the Prince of Peace, to our Savior who knelt to gather the slave's ear, brushed the dirt away, lifted it to the side of his flushed face. May we leave no scars. May we ask no blessing for the killing done in His name.

• • •

Coffins of Black

WILLIS BARNSTONE

A child's death cannot be explained.
I wonder why the lovely French girls
I saw in a Catholic hospital in Périgueux
lay unconscious on their beds
their faces gazing up at the ceiling.
The young faces seemed healthy,
a cancer raged inside.
They were not in pain, they were fully still.
In white gowns they lingered
in sun passing through the glass walls.
In stunning beauty and peace,
they ceased breathing and went
where no child should go,
where no child should go.

· · ·

We Are Seven

WILLIAM WORDSWORTH

—A simple Child,
That lightly draws its breath,
And feels its life in every limb,
What should it know of death?

I met a little cottage Girl:
She was eight years old, she said;
Her hair was thick with many a curl
That clustered round her head.

She had a rustic, woodland air,
And she was wildly clad:
Her eyes were fair, and very fair;
—Her beauty made me glad.

"Sisters and brothers, little Maid,
How many may you be?"
"How many? Seven in all," she said,
And wondering looked at me.

"And where are they? I pray you tell."
She answered, "Seven are we;
And two of us at Conway dwell,
And two are gone to sea.

"Two of us in the church-yard lie,
My sister and my brother;
And, in the church-yard cottage, I
Dwell near them with my mother."

"You say that two at Conway dwell,
And two are gone to sea,
Yet ye are seven! I pray you tell,
Sweet Maid, how this may be."

Then did the little Maid reply,
"Seven boys and girls are we;
Two of us in the church-yard lie,
Beneath the church-yard tree."

"You run about, my little Maid,
Your limbs they are alive;
If two are in the church-yard laid,
Then ye are only five."

"Their graves are green, they may be seen,"
The little Maid replied,
"Twelve steps or more from my mother's door,
And they are side by side.

"My stockings there I often knit,
My kerchief there I hem;
And there upon the ground I sit,
And sing a song to them.

"And often after sun-set, Sir,
When it is light and fair,
I take my little porringer,
And eat my supper there.

"The first that died was sister Jane;
In bed she moaning lay,
Till God released her of her pain;
And then she went away.

"So in the church-yard she was laid;
And, when the grass was dry,
Together round her grave we played,
My brother John and I.

"And when the ground was white with snow,
And I could run and slide,
My brother John was forced to go,
And he lies by her side."

"How many are you, then," said I,
"If they two are in heaven?"
Quick was the little Maid's reply,
"O Master! we are seven."

"But they are dead; those two are dead!
Their spirits are in heaven!"
'Twas throwing words away; for still
The little Maid would have her will,
And said, "Nay, we are seven!"

• • •

To My Cannibalized Twin

JENNIFER PERRINE

Whatever you were or might have been: orb,
lump, dim glow beside me, some human shard
of glitter, pearled sand in our mother's paunch:
I tell you now you were lucky, uncaged

by my misfit hunger. You can regard
it a kindness: my desire to absorb
has always been here, waiting to get drunk
on the next heart, imbibe a look through veiled

eyes, suck the tongue of somebody's pigtailed
beloved. Tell me, stranger, lonely monk
hovering somewhere in my cells, engaged

in whatever thankless task my young greed
assigned you: if you were here, could you staunch
this wanting, make me cough up its sharp seed?

• • •

To My Brother

W.S. MERWIN

Our mother wrote to you
before you were born
a note you might open
at some later date
in case she should not
be there to tell you
what was in her mind
about wanting you
when she had not seen you

74

that was before
my time and it
never turned out like that
you never saw the letter
and she never saw you
who were perfect they said
and dead within minutes
that far ahead
of me and always
looking the other way
and I would be the one
to open the letter
after she was gone

and you had answered it
without a word
before I was there
to find out about you
unseen elder
you perfect one
firstborn

•   •   •

Lines on His Brother's Grave

CATULLUS

O'er many a land and many a sea,
    My brother, I have come.
To pay the last sad rites to thee
    Upon thy silent tomb.
To speak to thee, ah, vain pretence!
Since cruel fate has snatched thee hence
    By most untimely doom,
Thine ashes dumb alone remain,
To me survives a lasting pain.

Meanwhile our father's rite of yore
    May now accomplished be.
Who to the grave sad offerings bore,
    So these accept from me.
Drenched with the tears of bitter woe
Such as a brother's heart can know
    The grief I feel for thee.
And now, all hail! my task is o'er.
Brother, farewell for evermore.

Translated from the Latin by T. Hart-Davies

• • •

Pronouncing the Dead

LORIE MISECK

. . . sister, there is no beginning, no end . . .
You have always been there, my birthmark
a scar on my heart, shape of a closed mouth.
A mouth tired of talking, singing.
A mouth tired of crying, explaining.
You have left an indelible mark,
an unfaded bruise I lean into.
            People don't die.

when the heart becomes silent,
when breath no longer swims through the body.
Pronouncing the dead is the last rite
of the living. When a phone call answered
splits the night, when a door opens to a
policeman dressed in apology.
            You did not die

alone in a hospital
with a hole in your pancreas,
round as the moon, size of an eye.
I did not pronounce you when

I picked up the phone
and mom's voice walked across glass,
words crawled from her emptied heart,
sought refuge in my ear.
                    You died

the last time I smelled you, drank you.
The last time I tasted you, at Christmas,
your hand brushing crumbs from my lips.
The last time our breath mixed together,
two clouds joining in cold air.
The last time we broke bread,
while stitching our wounded hearts into
doves ascending,
                    always ascending.

• • •

On the Death of Anne Brontë

Charlotte Brontë

There's little joy in life for me,
    And little terror in the grave;
I've lived the parting hour to see
    Of one I would have died to save.

Calmly to watch the failing breath,
    Wishing each sigh might be the last;
Longing to see the shade of death
    O'er those belovèd features cast.

The cloud, the stillness that must part
    The darling of my life from me;
And then to thank God from my heart,
    To thank Him well and fervently;

Although I knew that we had lost
    The hope and glory of our life;
And now, benighted, tempest-tossed,
    Must bear alone the weary strife.

• • •

To a Lady on the Death of Three Relations

PHILLIS WHEATLEY

We trace the pow'r of Death from tomb to tomb,
And his are all the ages yet to come.
'Tis his to call the planets from on high,
To blacken Phoebus, and dissolve the sky;
His too, when all in his dark realms are hurl'd,
From its firm base to shake the solid world;
His fatal sceptre rules the spacious whole,
And trembling nature rocks from pole to pole.
Awful he moves, and wide his wings are spread:

Behold thy brother number'd with the dead!
From bondage freed, the exulting spirit flies
Beyond Olympus, and these starry skies.
Lost in our woe for thee, blest shade, we mourn
In vain; to earth thou never must return.
Thy sisters too, fair mourner, feel the dart
Of Death, and with fresh torture rend thine heart.
Weep not for them, and leave the world behind.

As a young plant by hurricanes up torn,
So near its parent lies the newly born—
But 'midst the bright ethereal train behold
It shines superior on a throne of gold:
Then, mourner, cease; let hope thy tears restrain,
Smile on the tomb, and sooth the raging pain.
On yon blest regions fix thy longing view,

Mindless of sublunary scenes below;
Ascend the sacred mount, in thought arise,
And seek substantial and immortal joys;
Where hope receives, where faith to vision springs,
And raptur'd seraphs tune th' immortal strings
To strains ecstatic. Thou the chorus join,
And to thy father tune the praise divine.

• • •

A Single Autumn

W.S. MERWIN

The year my parents died
one that summer one that fall
three months and three days apart
I moved into the house
where they had lived their last years
it had never been theirs
and was still theirs in that way
for a while

echoes in every room
without a sound
all the things that we
had never been able to say
I could not remember

doll collection
in a china cabinet
plates stacked on shelves
lace on drop-leaf tables
a dried branch of bittersweet
before a hall mirror
were all planning to wait

the glass doors of the house
remained closed
the days had turned cold
and out in the tall hickories
the blaze of autumn had begun
on its own

I could do anything

• • •

"Full fathom five" (from *The Tempest*)

WILLIAM SHAKESPEARE

Full fathom five thy father lies;
Of his bones are coral made;
Those are pearls that were his eyes:
Nothing of him that doth fade
But doth suffer a sea-change
Into something rich and strange.
Sea-nymphs hourly ring his knell;
Hark! now I hear them—ding-dong, bell.

• • •

For Euthanasia and Pain-Killing Drugs

ALAN DUGAN

As my father died of cancer of the asshole
the doctor wouldn't give him habit-forming drugs
for fear of making him a hopeless addict
so it took two men to hold him down to die.
I ran around like crazy to the bars that day.
When I got back that night they said he died at noon,
so I squeezed out two tears because they said I should.

Look at what happened to your Uncle John they said.
He couldn't cry when Grandpa died
so he went nuts and tried to kill the priest.
We had to have him put away for life
but you are blessed, you cried, a good son,
you are saved, oh you are not your father's asshole,
may you never rot in shit, God bless your come.

· · ·

Lament

EDNA ST. VINCENT MILLAY

Listen, children:
Your father is dead.
From his old coats
I'll make you little jackets;
I'll make you little trousers
From his old pants.
There'll be in his pockets
Things he used to put there,
Keys and pennies
Covered with tobacco;
Dan shall have the pennies
To save in his bank;
Anne shall have the keys
To make a pretty noise with.
Life must go on,
And the dead be forgotten;
Life must go on,
Though good men die;
Anne, eat your breakfast;
Dan, take your medicine;
Life must go on;
I forget just why.

· · ·

To His Mother, C. L. M.

JOHN MASEFIELD

In the dark womb where I began
My mother's life made me a man.
Through all the months of human birth
Her beauty fed my common earth.
I cannot see, nor breathe, nor stir,
But through the death of some of her.

Down in the darkness of the grave
She cannot see the life she gave.
For all her love, she cannot tell
Whether I use it ill or well,
Nor knock at dusty doors to find
Her beauty dusty in the mind.

If the grave's gates could be undone,
She would not know her little son,
I am so grown. If we should meet,
She would pass by me in the street,
Unless my soul's face let her see
My sense of what she did for me.

What have I done to keep in mind
My debt to her and womankind?
What woman's happier life repays
Her for those months of wretched days?
For all my mouthless body leech'd
Ere Birth's releasing hell was reach'd?

What have I done, or tried, or said
In thanks to that dear woman dead?
Men triumph over women still,
Men trample women's rights at will,
And man's lust roves the world untamed.

O grave, keep shut lest I be shamed!

• • •

"oh antic God"

LUCILLE CLIFTON

oh antic God
return to me
my mother in her thirties
leaned across the front porch
the huge pillow of her breasts
pressing against the rail
summoning me in for bed.

I am almost the dead woman's age times two.

I can barely recall her song
the scent of her hands
though her wild hair scratches my dreams
at night.   return to me, oh Lord of then
and now, my mother's calling,
her young voice humming my name.

• • •

My Mother Contemplating Her Gun

NICK FLYNN

One boyfriend said to keep the bullets

>   *locked in a different room.*
>   *Another urged*
>   *clean it*
> *or it could explode. Larry*

thought I should keep it loaded
under my bed,
            you never know.

I bought it
when I didn't feel safe. The barrel
      is oily,

    reflective, the steel

pure, pulled from a hole
      in West Virginia. It

could have been cast into anything, nails
along the carpenter's lip, the ladder

to balance the train. Look at this, one
      bullet,

      how almost nothing it is—

    saltpeter   sulphur   lead   *Hell*

burns sulphur, a smell like this.
      safety & hammer, barrel & grip

    I don't know what I believe.

I remember the woods behind my father's house
      horses beside the quarry

stolen cars lost in the deepest wells,
the water below
      an ink waiting to fill me.

        Outside a towel hangs from a cold line
    a sheet of iron in the sky

    roses painted on it, blue roses.

Tomorrow it will still be there.

               •   •   •

To My Mother

W.S. MERWIN

This very evening I reach
the age you were when you died
I look through the decades
down past the layers of cloud
you had been watching the dark
autumn sky over the garden
and had told me months before
with a grace note of surprise
that you were an old woman
and you laughed at the sound of it
all my life you had told me
that dying did not frighten you
yours was the voice that told me
that I was not afraid
you stood up to go in
knowing it would rain that night

you had seen death many times
before I ever knew you
I am watching the rain now
fall on another garden
I hear your words in my head
it was the winter solstice
before I was thirty
that I was the age you had been
on the day I was born
to slip between numbers
through the measureless days

• • •

Time

KATERINA STOYKOVA-KLEMER

I asked Grandma
why she was crying.

She told me that
my great-grandmother Maria
her own mother
passed away.

"But that was last week!" I protested
frowned and pulled on her hand
to come play with me.

. . .

Aunt Helen

T.S. ELIOT

Miss Helen Slingsby was my maiden aunt,
And lived in a small house near a fashionable square
Cared for by servants to the number of four.
Now when she died there was silence in heaven
And silence at her end of the street.
The shutters were drawn and the undertaker wiped his feet—
He was aware that this sort of thing had occurred before.
The dogs were handsomely provided for,
But shortly afterwards the parrot died too.
The Dresden clock continued ticking on the mantelpiece,
And the footman sat upon the dining-table
Holding the second housemaid on his knees—
Who had always been so careful while her mistress lived.

. . .

For My Godmother, Twenty Years Later

STANLEY MOSS

Give me a death like hers without tears,
those flies on a summer day about a carcass—
about the house medicine, Mozart, and good cheer.
My song: life is short, art long, death longer.
My doctor uncle covered her with kisses.
When her life was a goldfinch in his hand,
on a feeder and birdbath outside her window:
larks sang, splashed and fed above the sparrows.
A blue jay militaire drove them away.
Then, a bird of prey, a necessary reprimand
screamed overhead without mercy. Instead
of terror, it was met at her window
by the warbler of good cheer that sometimes sings for the dead.
I whistle for it to come and nest near my window.

• • •

The Old Familiar Faces

CHARLES LAMB

I have had playmates, I have had companions,
In my days of childhood, in my joyful school-days,
All, all are gone, the old familiar faces.

I have been laughing, I have been carousing,
Drinking late, sitting late, with my bosom cronies,
All, all are gone, the old familiar faces.

I loved a love once, fairest among women;
Closed are her doors on me, I must not see her —
All, all are gone, the old familiar faces.

I have a friend, a kinder friend has no man;
Like an ingrate, I left my friend abruptly;
Left him, to muse on the old familiar faces.

Ghost-like, I paced round the haunts of my childhood.
Earth seemed a desert I was bound to traverse,
Seeking to find the old familiar faces.

Friend of my bosom, thou more than a brother,
Why wert not thou born in my father's dwelling?
So might we talk of the old familiar faces —

How some they have died, and some they have left me,
And some are taken from me; all are departed;
All, all are gone, the old familiar faces.

·   ·   ·

As From a Quiver of Arrows

CARL PHILLIPS

What do we do with the body, do we
burn it, do we set it in dirt or in
stone, do we wrap it in balm, honey,
oil, and then gauze and tip it onto
and trust it to a raft and to water?

What will happen to the memory of his
body, if one of us doesn't hurry now
and write it down fast? Will it be
salt or late light that it melts like?
Floss, rubber gloves, and a chewed cap

to a pen elsewhere—how are we to
regard his effects, do we throw them
or use them away, do we say they are
relics and so treat them like relics?
Does his soiled linen count? If so,

would we be wrong then, to wash it?
There are no instructions whether it
should go to where are those with no
linen, or whether by night we should
memorially wear it ourselves, by day

reflect upon it folded, shelved, empty.
Here, on the floor behind his bed is
a bent photo—why? Were the two of
them lovers? Does it mean, where we
found it, that he forgot it or lost it

or intended a safekeeping? Should we
attempt to make contact? What if this
other man too is dead? Or alive, but
doesn't want to remember, is human?
Is it okay to be human, and fall away

from oblation and memory, if we forget,
and can't sometimes help it and sometimes
it is all that we want? How long, in
dawns or new cocks, does that take?
What if it is rest and nothing else that

we want? Is it a findable thing, small?
In what hole is it hidden? Is it, maybe,
a country? Will a guide be required who
will say to us how? Do we fly? Do we
swim? What will I do now, with my hands?

• • •

From "To the Memory of Mrs. Lefroy who died Dec:r 16—My Birthday"

JANE AUSTEN

The day returns again, my natal day;
What mix'd emotions with the Thought arise!
Beloved friend, four years have pass'd away
Since thou wert snatch'd forever from our eyes.—
The day, commemorative of my birth
Bestowing Life and Light and Hope on me,
Brings back the hour which was thy last on Earth.
Oh! bitter pang of torturing Memory!—

• • •

The Letter

THOMAS BAILEY ALDRICH

I held his letter in my hand,
And even while I read
The lightning flashed across the land
The word that he was dead.
How strange it seemed! His living voice
Was speaking from the page
Those courteous phrases, tersely choice,
Light-hearted, witty, sage.

I wondered what it was that died!
The man himself was here,
His modesty, his scholar's pride,
His soul serene and clear.

These neither death nor time shall dim,
Still this sad thing must be—
Henceforth I may not speak to him,
Though he can speak to me!

• • •

Bess

WILLIAM STAFFORD

Ours are the streets where Bess first met her
cancer. She went to work every day past the
secure houses. At her job in the library
she arranged better and better flowers, and when
students asked for books her hand went out
to help. In the last year of her life
she had to keep her friends from knowing
how happy they were. She listened while they
complained about food or work or the weather.
And the great national events danced
their grotesque, fake importance. Always

Pain moved where she moved. She walked
ahead; it came. She hid; it found her.
No one ever served another so truly;
no enemy ever meant so strong a hate.
It was almost as if there was no room
left for her on earth. But she remembered
where joy used to live. She straightened its flowers;
she did not weep when she passed its houses;
and when finally she pulled into a tiny corner
and slipped from pain, her hand opened
again, and the streets opened, and she wished all well.

• • •

The Class of '69

SARAH FRELIGH

The legendary dead live on
in yearbooks of small town
high schools, black framed faces
airbrushed of acne, their eulogies

woven from the warp of truth,
the woof of exaggeration. Who
knew the girl that died of leukemia
swung snakes like lariats

and writhed with the fever
of Jesus on Sunday. Or the quiet boy
in the dark tie and starched shirt
whose head was sheared clean

from his neck one night when he drove
drunk under an oncoming semi.
Who knew he spent
his last hour throwing ten-dollar bills

at an old stripper named
Miss Cherry Blossom. Who knew
he laughed when she picked
them up in the crack of her ass.

Who knew how bad blood
cells multiply and gang up
on the good ones. Who knew
about Pavlov's dog, the tuning fork

and the promise of food. We lit
cigarettes and drove reckless
without seat belts. We screwed
without condoms and didn't

think twice about that bruise
on our leg, the arteries to our
hearts silting up with grease.
We bent over a light table

framing photos in small coffins
of black tape to honor
the legendary dead about
whom we knew nothing.

• • •

"Death sets a thing significant"

EMILY DICKINSON

Death sets a thing significant
The eye had hurried by,
Except a perished creature
Entreat us tenderly

To ponder little workmanships
In crayon or in wool,
With "This was last her fingers did,"
Industrious until

The thimble weighed too heavy,
The stitches stopped themselves,
And then 'twas put among the dust
Upon the closet shelves.

A book I have, a friend gave,
Whose pencil, here and there,
Had notched the place that pleased him,—
At rest his fingers are.

Now, when I read, I read not,
For interrupting tears
Obliterate the etchings
Too costly for repairs.

• • •

To an Athlete Dying Young

A.E. HOUSMAN

The time you won your town the race
We chaired you through the market-place;
Man and boy stood cheering by,
And home we brought you shoulder-high.

To-day, the road all runners come,
Shoulder-high we bring you home,
And set you at your threshold down,
Townsman of a stiller town.

Smart lad, to slip betimes away
From fields where glory does not stay
And early though the laurel grows
It withers quicker than the rose.

Eyes the shady night has shut
Cannot see the record cut,
And silence sounds no worse than cheers
After earth has stopped the ears:

Now you will not swell the rout
Of lads that wore their honours out,
Runners whom renown outran
And the name died before the man.

So set, before the echoes fade,
The fleet foot on the sill of shade,
And hold to the low lintel up
The still-defended challenge-cup.

And round that early-laurelled head
Will flock to gaze the strengthless dead,
And find unwithered on its curls
The garland briefer than a girl's.

• • •

"Oh! snatch'd away, in beauty's bloom,"

LORD BYRON

Oh! snatch'd away, in beauty's bloom,
On thee shall press no ponderous tomb;
  But on thy turf shall roses rear
  Their leaves, the earliest of the year;
And the wild cypress wave in tender gloom:

And oft by yon blue gushing stream
  Shall Sorrow lean her drooping head,
And feed deep thought with many a dream,
  And lingering pause and lightly tread;
  Fond wretch! as if her step disturb'd the dead!

Away! we know that tears are vain,
  That death nor heeds nor hears distress:
Will this unteach us to complain?
  Or make one mourner weep the less?
And thou—who tell'st me to forget,
Thy looks are wan, thine eyes are wet.

• • •

The Death-Bed

THOMAS HOOD

We watch'd her breathing thro' the night,
  Her breathing soft and low,
As in her breast the wave of life
  Kept heaving to and fro.

So silently we seem'd to speak,
  So slowly mov'd about,
As we had lent her half our powers
  To eke her living out.

Our very hopes belied our fears,
    Our fears our hopes belied—
We thought her dying when she slept,
    And sleeping when she died.

For when the morn came dim and sad,
    And chill with early showers,
Her quiet eyelids clos'd—she had
    Another morn than ours.

• • •

Dirge

ALFRED, LORD TENNYSON

Now is done thy long day's work;
Fold thy palms across thy breast,
Fold thine arms, turn to thy rest.
        Let them rave.
Shadows of the silver birk
Sweep the green that folds thy grave.
        Let them rave.

Thee nor carketh care nor slander;
Nothing but the small cold worm
Fretteth thine enshrouded form.
        Let them rave.
Light and shadow ever wander
O'er the green that folds thy grave.
        Let them rave.

Thou wilt not turn upon thy bed;
Chaunteth not the brooding bee
Sweeter tones than calumny?
        Let them rave.
Thou wilt never raise thine head
From the green that folds thy grave.
        Let them rave.

Crocodiles wept tears for thee;
The woodbine and eglatere
Drip sweeter dews than traitor's tear.
　　　Let them rave.
Rain makes music in the tree
O'er the green that folds thy grave.
　　　Let them rave.

Round thee blow, self-pleached deep,
Bramble-roses, faint and pale,
And long purples of the dale.
　　　Let them rave.
These in every shower creep
Thro' the green that folds thy grave.
　　　Let them rave.

The gold-eyed kingcups fine;
The frail bluebell peereth over
Rare broidry of the purple clover.
　　　Let them rave.
Kings have no such couch as thine,
As the green that folds thy grave.
　　　Let them rave.

Wild words wander here and there;
God's great gift of speech abused
Makes thy memory confused:
　　　But let them rave.
The balm-cricket carols clear
In the green that folds thy grave.
　　　Let them rave.

· · ·

after one year

LUCILLE CLIFTON

she who was beautiful
entered Lake-Too-Soon without warning us
that it would storm in
our hearts forever   that it would
alter the landscape of our lives
and that at night we would
fold ourselves into
towels into blankets anything
trying to stop our eyes
from drowning themselves

• • •

A Reminiscence

ANNE BRONTË

Yes, thou art gone! and never more
    Thy sunny smile shall gladden me;
But I may pass the old church door,
    And pace the floor that covers thee,

May stand upon the cold, damp stone,
    And think that, frozen, lies below
The lightest heart that I have known,
    The kindest I shall ever know.

Yet, though I cannot see thee more,
    'Tis still a comfort to have seen;
And though thy transient life is o'er,
    'Tis sweet to think that thou hast been;

To think a soul so near divine,
    Within a form so angel fair,
United to a heart like thine,
    Has gladdened once our humble sphere.

· · ·

The Passing of Arthur (from *Idylls of the King*)

ALFRED, LORD TENNYSON

  Then saw they how there hove a dusky barge,
Dark as a funeral scarf from stem to stern,
Beneath them; and descending they were ware
That all the decks were dense with stately forms,
Black-stol'd, black-hooded, like a dream—by these
Three Queens with crowns of gold: and from them rose
A cry that shiver'd to the tingling stars,
And, as it were one voice, an agony
Of lamentation, like a wind that shrills
All night in a waste land, where no one comes,
Or hath come, since the making of the world.

    Then murmur'd Arthur, "Place me in the barge."
So to the barge they came. There those three Queens
Put forth their hands, and took the King, and wept.
But she, that rose the tallest of them all
And fairest, laid his head upon her lap,
And loos'd the shatter'd casque, and chaf'd his hands,
And call'd him by his name, complaining loud,
And dropping bitter tears against a brow
Strip'd with dark blood: for all his face was white
And colorless, and like the wither'd moon
Smote by the fresh beam of the springing east;
And all his greaves and cuisses dash'd with drops
Of onset; and the light and lustrous curls—
That made his forehead like a rising sun
High from the dais-throne—were parch'd with dust;

Or, clotted into points and hanging loose,
Mix'd with the knightly growth that fringed his lips.
So like a shatter'd column lay the King;
Not like that Arthur who, with lance in rest,
From spur to plume a star of tournament,
Shot thro' the lists at Camelot, and charged
Before the eyes of ladies and of kings.

•   •   •

Richard Cory

EDWIN ARLINGTON ROBINSON

Whenever Richard Cory went down town,
We people on the pavement looked at him:
He was a gentleman from sole to crown,
Clean favored, and imperially slim.

And he was always quietly arrayed,
And he was always human when he talked;
But still he fluttered pulses when he said,
"Good-morning," and he glittered when he walked.

And he was rich—yes, richer than a king—
And admirably schooled in every grace:
In fine, we thought that he was everything
To make us wish that we were in his place.

So on we worked, and waited for the light,
And went without the meat, and cursed the bread;
And Richard Cory, one calm summer night,
Went home and put a bullet through his head.

•   •   •

The Ballad of Dead Ladies

FRANÇOIS VILLON

Tell me now in what hidden way is
　Lady Flora the lovely Roman?
Where's Hipparchia, and where is Thais,
　Neither of them the fairer woman
　Where is Echo, beheld of no man,
Only heard on river and mere,—
　She whose beauty was more than human? . . .
But where are the snows of yester-year?

Where's Héloise, the learned nun,
　For whose sake Abeillard, I ween,
Lost manhood and put priesthood on?
　(From Love he won such dule and teen!)
　And where, I pray you, is the Queen
Who will'd that Buridan should steer
　Sew'd in a sack's mouth down the Seine? . . .
But where are the snows of yester-year?
　White Queen Blanche, like a queen of lilies,
　With a voice like any mermaiden,—
Bertha Broadfoot, Beatrice, Alice,
　And Ermengarde the lady of Maine,—
　And that good Joan whom English-men
At Rouen doom'd and burn'd her there,—
　Mother of God, where are they then? . . .
But where are the snows of yester-year?

Nay, never ask this week, fair lord,
　Where they are gone, nor yet this year,
Save with thus much for an overword,—
　But where are the snows of yester-year?

Translated from the French by Dante Gabriel Rossetti

•　•　•

Death by Water (from *The Waste Land*)

T.S. ELIOT

Phlebas the Phoenician, a fortnight dead,
Forgot the cry of gulls, and the deep sea swell
And the profit and loss.
          A current under sea
Picked his bones in whispers. As he rose and fell
He passed the stages of his age and youth
Entering the whirlpool.
          Gentile or Jew
O you who turn the wheel and look to windward,
Consider Phlebas, who was once handsome and tall as you.

. . .

To Cruel Ocean

VICTOR HUGO

Where are the hapless shipmen?—disappeared,
  Gone down, where witness none, save Night, hath been,
Ye deep, deep waves, of kneeling mothers feared,
  What dismal tales know ye of things unseen?
  Tales that ye tell your whispering selves between
    The while in clouds to the flood-tide ye pour;
  And this it is that gives you, as I ween,
    Those mournful voices, mournful evermore,
    When ye come in at eve to us who dwell on shore.

Translated from the French by Huntington Smith

. . .

From *Lycidas*

JOHN MILTON

Yet once more, O ye Laurels, and once more
Ye Myrtles brown, with Ivy never-sear,
I com to pluck your Berries harsh and crude,
And with forc'd fingers rude,
Shatter your leaves before the mellowing year.
Bitter constraint, and sad occasion dear,
Compels me to disturb your season due:
For Lycidas is dead, dead ere his prime!
Young Lycidas, and hath not left his peer:
Who would not sing for Lycidas? he knew
Himself to sing, and build the lofty rhyme.
He must not flote upon his watry bear
Unwept, and welter to the parching wind,
Without the meed of som melodious tear.

*

  But O the heavy change, now thou art gon,
Now thou art gon, and never must return!
Thee Shepherd, thee the Woods, and desert Caves,
With wilde Thyme and the gadding Vine o'regrown,
And all their echoes mourn.
The Willows, and the Hazle Copses green,
Shall now no more be seen,
Fanning their joyous Leaves to thy soft layes.
As killing as the Canker to the Rose,
Or Taint-worm to the weanling Herds that graze,
Or Frost to Flowers, that their gay wardrop wear,
When first the White thorn blows;
Such, Lycidas, thy loss to Shepherd's ear.

• • •

Epitaph on the Countess Dowager of Pembroke

WILLIAM BROWNE OF TAVISTOCK

Underneath this sable hearse
Lies the subject of all verse,
Sidney's sister, Pembroke's mother.
Death, ere thou hast slain another
Fair and learned and good as she,
Time shall throw a dart at thee.

• • •

"O Sorrow" (from *Endymion*)

JOHN KEATS

O Sorrow,
    Why dost borrow
The natural hue of health, from vermeil lips?—
    To give maiden blushes
    To the white rose bushes?
Or is't thy dewy hand the daisy tips?

O Sorrow,
    Why dost borrow
The lustrous passion from a falcon-eye?—
    To give the glow-worm light?
    Or, on a moonless night,
To tinge, on syren shores, the salt sea-spry?

O Sorrow,
    Why dost borrow
The mellow ditties from a mourning tongue?—
    To give at evening pale
    Unto the nightingale,
That thou mayst listen the cold dews among?

O Sorrow,
   Why dost borrow
Heart's lightness from the merriment of May?—
   A lover would not tread
   A cowslip on the head,
Though he should dance from eve till peep of day—
   Nor any drooping flower
   Held sacred for thy bower,
Wherever he may sport himself and play.

   To Sorrow
I bade good morrow,
And thought to leave her far away behind;
   But cheerly, cheerly,
   She loves me dearly;
She is so constant to me, and so kind:
   I would deceive her,
   And so leave her,
But ah! she is so constant and so kind.

*

   Come then, Sorrow!
   Sweetest Sorrow!
Like an own babe I nurse thee on my breast:
   I thought to leave thee
   And deceive thee,
But now of all the world I love thee best.

• • •

From "Adonais: An Elegy on the Death of John Keats"

PERCY BYSSHE SHELLEY

I weep for Adonais—he is dead!
   O, weep for Adonais! though our tears
   Thaw not the frost which binds so dear a head!
   And thou, sad Hour, selected from all years
   To mourn our loss, rouse thy obscure compeers,
   And teach them thine own sorrow! Say: "With me
   Died Adonais; till the Future dares
   Forget the Past, his fate and fame shall be
An echo and a light unto eternity!"

*

Peace, peace! he is not dead, he doth not sleep—
   He hath awakened from the dream of life—
   'Tis we, who lost in stormy visions, keep
   With phantoms an unprofitable strife,
   And in mad trance, strike with our spirit's knife
   Invulnerable nothings.—We decay
   Like corpses in a charnel; fear and grief
   Convulse us and consume us day by day,
And cold hopes swarm like worms within our living clay.

*

He is made one with Nature: there is heard
   His voice in all her music, from the moan
   Of thunder, to the song of night's sweet bird;
   He is a presence to be felt and known
   In darkness and in light, from herb and stone,
   Spreading itself where'er that Power may move
   Which has withdrawn his being to its own;
   Which wields the world with never wearied love,
Sustains it from beneath, and kindles it above.

•   •   •

Epitaphs

ROBERT BURNS

Epitaph on James Grieve

Here lies Boghead amang the dead
  In hopes to get salvation;
But if such as he in Heav'n may be,
  Then welcome, hail! damnation.

Epitaph on a Henpecked Squire

As father Adam first was fool'd,
  (A case that's still too common,)
Here lies man a woman ruled,
  The devil ruled the woman.

Epitaph for James Smith

Lament him, Mauchline husbands a',
  He aften did assist ye;
For had ye staid hale weeks awa,
  Your wives they ne'er had miss'd ye.

Ye Mauchline bairns [i.e., children], as on ye press
  To school in bands thegither,
O tread ye lightly on his grass,—
  Perhaps he was your father!

Epitaph on a Noted Coxcomb

Capt. Wm. Roddirk, of Corbiston.

Light lay the earth on Billy's breast,
  His chicken heart so tender;
But build a castle on his head,
  His scull will prop it under.

Epitaph on Wm. Graham, Esq., of Mossknowe

"Stop thief!" dame Nature call'd to Death,
As Willy drew his latest breath;
How shall I make a fool again?
My choicest model thou hast ta'en.

. . .

"The bustle in a house"

EMILY DICKINSON

The bustle in a house
The morning after death
Is solemnest of industries
Enacted upon earth,—

The sweeping up the heart,
And putting love away
We shall not want to use again
Until eternity.

. . .

"The days of Spring are here!"

HAFIZ

The days of Spring are here! the eglantine,
The rose, the tulip from the dust have risen—
And thou, why liest thou beneath the dust?
Like the full clouds of Spring, these eyes of mine
Shall scatter tears upon the grave thy prison,
Till thou too from the earth thine head shalt thrust.

Translated from the Persian by Getrude Lowthian Bell

. . .

The Bones of the Dead

GABRIELA MISTRAL

The bones of the dead are tender ice
that knows how to crumble
and become dust on the lips
of the ones who loved them.
And these live lips can no longer kiss.

The bones of the dead
swiftly
spread their whiteness
over life's intense flame.
They kill all passion!

The bones of the dead
can do more than living flesh.
Even disjointed, they make mighty chains,
keeping us submissive and captive.

Translated from the Spanish by Maria Giachetti

•   •   •

The Letters of the Dead

WISLAWA SZYMBORSKA

We read the letters of the dead like helpless gods,
but gods, nonetheless, since we know the dates that follow.
We know which debts will never be repaid.
Which widows will remarry with the corpse still warm.
Poor dead, blindfolded dead,
gullible, fallible, pathetically prudent.
We see the faces people make behind their backs.
We catch the sound of wills being ripped to shreds.
The dead sit before us comically, as if on buttered bread,
or frantically pursue the hats blown from their heads.

Their bad taste, Napoleon, steam, electricity,
their fatal remedies for curable diseases,
their foolish apocalypse according to St. John,
their counterfeit heaven on earth according to Jean-Jacques. . . .
We watch the pawns on their chessboards in silence,
even though we see them three squares later.
Everything the dead predicted has turned out completely different.
Or a little bit different—which is to say, completely different.
The most fervent of them gaze confidingly into our eyes:
their calculations tell them that they'll find perfection there.

Translated from the Polish by Stanislaw Barańczak and Clare Cavanagh

• • •

To the Forgotten Dead

MARGARET L. WOODS

To the forgotten dead,
Come, let us drink in silence ere we part.
To every fervent yet resolvèd heart
That brought its tameless passion and its tears,
Renunciation and laborious years,
To lay the deep foundations of our race,
To rear its mighty ramparts overhead
And light its pinnacles with golden grace.
To the unhonoured dead.

To the forgotten dead,
Whose dauntless hands were stretched to grasp the rein
Of Fate and hurl into the void again
Her thunder-hoofèd horses, rushing blind
Earthward along the courses of the wind.
Among the stars, along the wind in vain
Their souls were scattered and their blood was shed,
And nothing, nothing of them doth remain.
To the thrice-perished dead.

• • •

If You Knew

ELLEN BASS

What if you knew you'd be the last
to touch someone?
If you were taking tickets, for example,
at the theater, tearing them,
giving back the ragged stubs,
you might take care to touch that palm,
brush your fingertips
along the life line's crease.

When a man pulls his wheeled suitcase
too slowly through the airport, when
the car in front of me doesn't signal,
when the clerk at the pharmacy
won't say *Thank you,* I don't remember
they're going to die.

A friend told me she'd been with her aunt.
They'd just had lunch and the waiter,
a young gay man with plum black eyes,
joked as he served the coffee, kissed
her aunt's powdered cheek when they left.
Then they walked half a block and her aunt
dropped dead on the sidewalk.

How close does the dragon's spume
have to come? How wide does the crack
in heaven have to split?
What would people look like
if we could see them as they are,
soaked in honey, stung and swollen,
reckless, pinned against time?

love

In which the poets prove that love is stronger than death . . . mostly

If Death Is Kind

SARA TEASDALE

Perhaps if Death is kind, and there can be returning,
  We will come back to earth some fragrant night,
And take these lanes to find the sea, and bending
  Breathe the same honeysuckle, low and white.

We will come down at night to these resounding beaches
  And the long gentle thunder of the sea,
Here for a single hour in the wide starlight
  We shall be happy, for the dead are free.

• • •

And You as Well Must Die

EDNA ST. VINCENT MILLAY

And you as well must die, belovèd dust,
And all your beauty stand you in no stead;
This flawless, vital hand, this perfect head,
This body of flame and steel, before the gust
Of Death, or under his autumnal frost,
Shall be as any leaf, be no less dead
Than the first leaf that fell,—this wonder fled,
Altered, estranged, disintegrated, lost.
Nor shall my love avail you in your hour.
In spite of all my love, you will arise
Upon that day and wander down the air
Obscurely as the unattended flower,
It mattering not how beautiful you were,
Or how belovèd above all else that dies.

• • •

From "A Boy's Poem"

ALEXANDER SMITH

We bury Love,
Forgetfulness grows over it like grass;
That is a thing to weep for, not the dead.

• • •

untitled poem

ALAN DUGAN

Why feel guilty because the death of a lover causes lust?
It is only an animal urge to perpetuate the species,
but if I do not inhibit my imagination and dreams
I can see your skull smiling up at me from underground
and your bones loosely arranged in the missionary position.
This is not an incapacitating vision except at night,
and not a will of constancy, nor an irrevocable trust,
so I take on a woman with a mouth like an open wound.
I would do almost anything to avoid your teeth in the dirt.
She is desirable, loving, and definite, but when I feel her up
I hesitate: I still feel the size of your absence. It is
as large as the silence of your invitational smile
or the vacancy open in the cage of your ribs. Fuck that,
I say. Why be guilty for this guilt? It's only birth control.
Therefore I extend my hands tongue and prick to you
through her as substitutions for the rest of my body
in hopes that you'll be born again as her daughter
before I have to join you as your permanent husband,
but I know you: you want me to come, come as I am,
right now, without her, and to bring along a son.

• • •

Oneness

THÍCH NHẤT HẠNH

The moment I die,
I will try to come back to you
as quickly as possible.
I promise it will not take long.
Isn't it true
I am already with you,
as I die each moment?
I come back to you
in every moment.
Just look,
feel my presence.
If you want to cry,
please cry.
And know
that I will cry with you.
The tears you shed
will heal us both.
Your tears are mine.
The earth I tread this morning
transcends history.
Spring and Winter are both present in the moment.
The young leaf and the dead leaf are really one.
My feet touch deathlessness,
and my feet are yours.
Walk with me now.
Let us enter the dimension of oneness
and see the cherry tree blossom in Winter.
Why should we talk about death?
I don't need to die
to be back with you.

. . .

Dead Love

MARY MATHEWS ADAMS

Two loves had I. Now both are dead,
  And both are marked by tombstones white.
The one stands in the churchyard near,
  The other hid from mortal sight.

The name on one all men may read,
  And learn who lies beneath the stone;
The other name is written where
  No eyes can read it but my own.

On one I plant a living flower,
  And cherish it with loving hands;
I shun the single withered leaf
  That tells me where the other stands.

To that white tombstone on the hill
  In summer days I often go;
From this white stone that nearer lies
  I turn me with unuttered woe.

O God, I pray, if love must die,
  And make no more of life a part,
Let witness be where all can see,
  And not within a living heart.

• • •

Spooks

C.S. LEWIS

Last night I dreamed that I was come again
Unto the house where my beloved dwells
After long years of wandering and pain.

And I stood out beneath the drenching rain
And all the street was bare, and black with night,
But in my true love's house was warmth and light.

Yet I could not draw near nor enter in,
And long I wondered if some secret sin
Or old, unhappy anger held me fast;

Till suddenly it came into my head
That I was killed long since and lying dead—
Only a homeless wraith that way had passed.

So thus I found my true love's house again
And stood unseen amid the winter night
And the lamp burned within, a rosy light,
And the wet street was shining in the rain.

• • •

Requiem

CHRISTINA ROSSETTI

When I am dead, my dearest,
Sing no sad songs for me;
Plant thou no roses at my head,
Nor shady cypress tree:
Be the green grass above me
With showers and dewdrops wet;
And if thou wilt, remember,
And if thou wilt, forget.

I shall not see the shadows,
I shall not feel the rain;
I shall not hear the nightingale
Sing on, as if in pain:
And dreaming through the twilight
That doth not rise nor set,
Haply I may remember,
And haply may forget.

. . .

Testament

HAYDEN CARRUTH

So often it has been displayed to us, the hourglass
with its grains of sand drifting down,
not as an object in our world
but as a sign, a symbol, our lives
drifting down grain by grain,
sifting away — I'm sure everyone must
see this emblem somewhere in the mind.
Yet not only our lives drift down. The stuff
of ego with which we began, the mass
in the upper chamber, filters away
as love accumulates below. Now
I am almost entirely love. I have been
to the banker, the broker, those strange
people, to talk about unit trusts,
annuities, CDs, IRAs, trying
to leave you whatever I can after
I die. I've made my will, written
you a long letter of instructions.
I think about this continually.
What will you do? How
will you live? You can't go back
to cocktail waitressing in the casino.
And your poetry? It will bring you

at best a pittance in our civilization,
a widow's mite, as mine has
for forty-five years. Which is why
I leave you so little. Brokers?
Unit trusts? I'm no financier doing
the world's great business. And the sands
in the upper glass grow few. Can I leave
you the vale of ten thousand trilliums
where we buried our good cat Pokey
across the lane to the quarry?
Maybe the tulips I planted under
the lilac tree? Or our red-bellied
woodpeckers who have given us so
much pleasure, and the rabbits
and the deer? And kisses? And
love-makings? All our embracings?
I know millions of these will be still
unspent when the last grain of sand
falls with its whisper, its inconsequence,
on the mountain of my love below.

•   •   •

A Grave Song

AMY LOWELL

I've a pocketful of emptiness for you, my Dear.
I've a heart like a loaf was baked yesteryear,
I've a mind like ashes spilt a week ago,
I've a hand like a rusty, cracked corkscrew.

Can you flourish on nothing and find it good?
Can you make petrification do for food?
Can you warm yourself at ashes on a stone?
Can you give my hand the cunning which has gone?

If you can, I will go and lay me down
And kiss the edge of your purple gown.
I will rise and walk with the sun on my head.
Will you walk with me, will you follow the dead?

. . .

Love and Death

MARGARET DELAND

Alas! that men must see
   Love, before Death!
Else they content might be
   With their short breath;
Aye, glad, when the pale sun
Showed restless Day was done,
And endless Rest begun.

Glad, when with strong, cool hand
   Death clasped their own,
And with a strange command
   Hushed every moan;
Glad to have finished pain,
And labor wrought in vain,
Blurred by Sin's deepening stain.

But Love's insistent voice
   Bids Self to flee—
"Live that I may rejoice,
   Live on, for me!"
So, for Love's cruel mind,
Men fear this Rest to find,
Nor know great Death is kind!

. . .

Unheard Melodies

SAPPHO

A tune for you, girls,
each one of you more delicious than the gifts of the muses;
heed my song, this lyre's sad *plink* not the half of it:

This poor wood thing—like *this* wood thing, my body,
dried, its fine black strings now all gone white.

Desire trudges to catch up, no matter how slow ahead I plod,
on gams that once weaved dances, as taut and light as gamboling fawns'.

What's left, but to complain? Remedies are gone:
woman, like man, grows old.

The goddess of Dawn fell in love once, with mortal Tithonus,
and the goddess planned ahead: Zeus,
make him immortal, she pled.
He did, granted life eternal,

but no one said anything about equally enduring youth.
Tithonus grew old, older, really, than time,
a groaning, feeble, nasty but living corpse.
She shut him away after just a century—

Open his door a crack: his moaning is this song.

Translated from the Greek by Kent H. Dixon

• • •

Troth with the Dead

D.H. LAWRENCE

The moon is broken in twain, and half a moon
Before me lies on the still, pale floor of the sky;

The other half of the broken coin of troth
Is buried away in the dark, where the still dead lie.
They buried her half in the grave when they laid her
    away;
I had pushed it gently in among the thick of her hair
Where it gathered towards the plait, on that very
    last day;
And like a moon in secret it is shining there.

My half shines in the sky, for a general sign
Of the troth with the dead I pledged myself to keep;
Turning its broken edge to the dark, it shines indeed
Like the sign of a lover who turns to the dark of
    sleep.
Against my heart the inviolate sleep breaks still
In darkened waves whose breaking echoes o'er
The wondering world of my wakeful day, till I'm
    lost
In the midst of the places I knew so well before.

• • •

From "The Apparition"

STEPHEN PHILLIPS

My dead Love came to me, and said
"God gives me one hour's rest,
To spend upon the earth with thee:
How shall we spend it best?"

"Why as of old," I said, and so
We quarrelled as of old.
But when I turned to make my peace,
That one short hour was told.

• • •

I Want to Die While You Love Me

GEORGIA DOUGLAS JOHNSON

I want to die while you love me,
  While yet you hold me fair,
While laughter lies upon my lips
  And lights are in my hair.

I want to die while you love me,
  And bear to that still bed,
Your kisses turbulent, unspent
  To warm me when I'm dead.

I want to die while you love me
  Oh, who would care to live
Till love has nothing more to ask
  And nothing more to give!

I want to die while you love me
  And never, never see
The glory of this perfect day
  Grow dim or cease to be.

• • •

Sonnet 66

WILLIAM SHAKESPEARE

Tir'd with all these, for restful death I cry
As to behold desert a beggar born,
And needy nothing trimm'd in jollity,
And purest faith unhappily forsworn,
And gilded honour shamefully misplac'd,
And maiden virtue rudely strumpeted,
And right perfection wrongfully disgraced,
And strength by limping sway disabled,
And art made tongue-tied by authority,

And folly—doctor-like—controlling skill,
And simple truth miscall'd simplicity,
And captive good attending captain ill:
　　Tir'd with all these, from these would I be gone,
　　Save that, to die, I leave my love alone.

•　•　•

The Lament of the Border Widow

TRADITIONAL ENGLISH BALLAD

My love he built me a bonny bower,
And clad it a' wi' lily flower;
A brawer bower ye ne'er did see,
Than my true love he built for me.

There came a man, by middle day,
He spied his sport, and went away;
And brought the King that very night,
Who brake my bower, and slew my knight.

He slew my knight, to me so dear;
He slew my knight, and took his gear;
My servants all for life did flee,
And left me in extremity.

I sew'd his sheet, making my mane;
I watch'd the corpse, myself alone;
I watch'd his body, night and day;
No living creature came that way.

I took his body on my back,
And whiles I gaed, and whiles I sat;
I digg'd a grave, and laid him in,
And happ'd him with the sod so green.

But think not ye my heart was sore,
When I laid the mol' on his yellow hair;
O think not ye my heart was woe,
When I turn'd about, away to go?

No living man I'll love again,
Since that my lovely knight is slain;
Wi' a lock of his yellow hair
I'll chain my heart for evermore.

. . .

Annabel Lee

EDGAR ALLAN POE

It was many and many a year ago,
    In a kingdom by the sea,
That a maiden lived whom you may know
    By the name of Annabel Lee; —
And this maiden she lived with no other thought
    Than to love and be loved by me.

She was a child and *I* was a child,
    In this kingdom by the sea,
But we loved with a love that was more than love —
    I and my Annabel Lee —
With a love that the wingéd seraphs of Heaven
    Coveted her and me.

And this was the reason that, long ago,
    In this kingdom by the sea,
A wind blew out of a cloud by night
    Chilling my Annabel Lee;
So that her high-born kinsmen came
    And bore her away from me,
To shut her up, in a sepulchre
    In this kingdom by the sea.

The angels, not half so happy in Heaven,
    Went envying her and me;
Yes! that was the reason (as all men know,
    In this kingdom by the sea)
That the wind came out of the cloud, chilling
    And killing my Annabel Lee.

But our love it was stronger by far than the love
    Of those who were older than we —
    Of many far wiser than we —
And neither the angels in Heaven above
    Nor the demons down under the sea
Can ever dissever my soul from the soul
    Of the beautiful Annabel Lee: —

For the moon never beams without bringing me dreams
    Of the beautiful Annabel Lee;
And the stars never rise but I see the bright eyes
    Of the beautiful Annabel Lee;
And so, all the night-tide, I lie down by the side
Of my darling, my darling, my life and my bride
    In her sepulchre there by the sea —
    In her tomb by the side of the sea.

• • •

To a Dead Lover

LOUISE BOGAN

The dark is thrown
Back from the brightness, like hair
Cast over a shoulder.
I am alone,

Four years older;
Like the chairs and the walls
Which I once watched brighten
With you beside me. I was to waken
Never like this, whatever came or was taken.

The stalk grows, the year beats on the wind.
Apples come, and the month for their fall.
The bark spreads, the roots tighten.
Though today be the last
Or tomorrow all,
You will not mind.

That I may not remember
Does not matter.
I shall not be with you again.
What we knew, even now
Must scatter
And be ruined, and blow
Like dust in the rain.

You have been dead a long season
And have less than desire
Who were lover with lover;
And I have life—that old reason
To wait for what comes,
To leave what is over.

· · ·

"Grieve not, dear Love!"

JOHN DIGBY, EARL OF BRISTOL

Grieve not, dear Love! although we often part:
   But know, that Nature gently doth us sever,
Thereby to train us up, with tender art,
   To brook the day when we must part for ever.

For Nature, doubting we should be surprised
   By that sad day whose dread doth chiefly fear us,
Doth keep us daily schooled and exercised;
   Lest that the fright thereof should overbear us!

· · ·

Upon the Death of Sir Albertus Morton's Wife

SIR HENRY WOTTON

He first deceas'd; she for a little tried
To live without him,—lik'd it not, and died.

. . .

From "The Relique"

JOHN DONNE

When my grave is broke up again
Some second guest to entertain, . . .
And he that digs it, spies
A bracelet of bright hair about the bone,
Will he not let us alone,
And think that there a loving couple lies,
Who thought that this device might be some way
To make their souls, at the last busy day,
Meet at this grave, and make a little stay?

. . .

Love And Death

ALFRED, LORD TENNYSON

What time the mighty moon was gathering light
Love paced the thymy plots of Paradise,
And all about him roll'd his lustrous eyes;
When, turning round a cassia, full in view,
Death, walking all alone beneath a yew,
And talking to himself, first met his sight:
"You must begone," said Death, "these walks are mine."
Love wept and spread his sheeny vans for flight;
Yet ere he parted said, "This hour is thine:
Thou art the shadow of life, and as the tree

Stands in the sun and shadows all beneath,
So in the light of great eternity
Life eminent creates the shade of death;
The shadow passeth when the tree shall fall,
But I shall reign for ever over all."

• • •

A Quoi Bon Dire

CHARLOTTE MEW

Seventeen years ago you said
   Something that sounded like Good-bye;
   And everybody thinks that you are dead,
      But I.

   So I, as I grow stiff and cold
To this and that say Good-bye too;
   And everybody sees that I am old
      But you.

   And one fine morning in a sunny lane
Some boy and girl will meet and kiss and swear
   That nobody can love their way again
      While over there
You will have smiled, I shall have tossed your hair.

• • •

An Epitaph upon Husband and Wife
Who died and were buried together

RICHARD CRASHAW

To these whom death again did wed
This grave's the second marriage-bed.
For though the hand of Fate could force

'Twixt soul and body a divorce,
It could not sever man and wife,
Because they both lived but one life.
Peace, good reader, do not weep;
Peace, the lovers are asleep.
They, sweet turtles, folded lie
In the last knot that love could tie.
Let them sleep, let them sleep on,
Till the stormy night be gone,
And the eternal morrow dawn;
Then the curtains will be drawn,
And they wake into a light
Whose day shall never die in night.

. . .

"I Have No Wealth of Grief"

LUCY KNOX

I have no wealth of grief; no sobs, no tears,
   Not any sighs, no words, no overflow
   Nor storms of passion, no reliefs; yet oh!
I have a leaden grief, and with it fears
Lest they who think there's nought where nought appears
   May say I never loved him. Ah not so!
   Love for him fills my heart; if grief is slow
In utterance, remember that for years
Love was a habit and the grief is new,
   So new a thing it has no language yet.
   Tears crowd my heart: with eyes that are not wet
I watch the rain-drops, silent, large, and few,
   Blotting a stone; then, comforted, I take
   Those drops to be my tears, shed for his sake.

. . .

Quanta invidia io ti porto

PETRARCH

O Earth, whose clay-cold mantle shrouds that face
  And veils those eyes that late so brightly shone,
  Whence all that gave delight on Earth was known;
How much I envy thee that harsh embrace!

O Heaven, that in thy airy Courts confin'd
  That purest Spirit when from Earth she fled
  And sought the Mansions of the righteous Dead,—
Ah envious, thus to leave my parting Soul behind!

O Angels that in your seraphic Choir
  Receiv'd her Sister-soul, and now enjoy
  Still present these Delights without alloy
Which my fond Heart must still in vain desire!
In Her I liv'd; in her my Life decays:—
Yet envious Fate denies to end my hapless days.

Translated from the Italian by Robert Cadell

• • •

"Life Knows No Dead So Beautiful"

JOAQUIN MILLER

Life knows no dead so beautiful
As is the white cold coffin'd past;
This I may love nor be betray'd:
The dead are faithful to the last.
I am not spouseless—I have wed
A memory—a life that's dead.

• • •

132

On His Deceased Wife

JOHN MILTON

Methought I saw my late espoused Saint
Brought to me like Alcestis from the grave,
  Whom Jove's great Son to her glad Husband gave,
  Rescu'd from death by force though pale and faint.
Mine as whom washt from spot of child-bed taint,
    Purification in the old Law did save,
    And such, as yet once more I trust to have
    Full sight of her in Heaven without restraint,
Came vested all in white, pure as her mind:
    Her face was veil'd, yet to my fancied sight,
    Love, sweetness, goodness, in her person shin'd
So clear, as in no face with more delight.
    But O as to embrace me she inclin'd
    I wak'd, she fled, and day brought back my night.

· · ·

Keen

EDNA ST. VINCENT MILLAY

Weep him dead and mourn as you may,
    Me, I sing as I must:
Blessèd be Death, that cuts in marble
    What would have sunk to dust!

Blessèd be Death, that took my love
    And buried him in the sea,
Where never a lie nor a bitter word
    Will out of his mouth at me.

This I have to hold to my heart,
    This to take by the hand:
Sweet we were for a summer month
    As the sun on the dry white sand;

Mild we were for a summer month
   As the wind from over the weirs.
And blessèd be Death, that hushed with salt
   The harsh and slovenly years!

Who builds her a house with love for timber
   Builds her a house of foam.
And I'd liefer be bride to a lad gone down
   Than widow to one safe home.

· · ·

Seraphine

HEINRICH HEINE

In the dreamy wood I wander,
   In the wood at eventide;
And thy slender graceful figure
   Wanders ever by my side.

Is not this thy white veil floating,
   Is not that thy gentle face?
Is it but the moonlight breaking
   Through the dark fir branches' space?

Can these tears so softly flowing
   Be my very own I hear?
Or indeed, art thou beside me,
   Weeping, darling, close anear?

Translated from the German by Emma Lazarus

· · ·

The Vinegar Man

RUTH COMFORT MITCHELL

The crazy old Vinegar Man is dead! He never had missed a day before!
Somebody went to his tumble-down shed by the Haunted House and forced
    the door.
There in the litter of his pungent pans, the murky mess of his mixing place—
Deep, sticky spiders and empty cans—with the same old frown on his sour
    old face.

    "Vinegar-Vinegar-Vinegar Man!
    Face-us-and-chase-us-and-catch-if-you-can!
    Pepper for a tongue! Pickle for a nose!
    Stick a pin in him and vinegar flows!
    Glare-at-us-swear-at-us-catch-if-you-can!
    Ketchup-and-chow-chow-and-Vinegar-Man!"

Nothing but recipes and worthless junk; greasy old records of paid and due;
But down in the depths of a battered trunk, a queer, quaint Valentine torn in
    two—
Red hearts and arrows and silver lace, and a prim, dim, ladylike script that said—
(Oh, Vinegar Man with the sour old face!)—"With dearest love, from Ellen
    to Ned!"

    "Steal-us-and-peel-us-and-drown-us-in-brine!
    He pickles his heart in"—a *valentine!*
    "Vinegar for blood! Pepper for his tongue!
    Stick a pin in him and"— *once he was young!*
    "Glare-at-us-swear-at-us-catch-if-you-can!"—
    "With dearest love"—*to the Vinegar Man!*

Dingy little books of profit and loss (died about Saturday, so they say),
And a queer, quaint valentine torn across . . . torn, but it never was thrown
    away!
"With dearest love from Ellen to Ned"— "Old Pepper Tongue! Pickles his
    heart in brine!"
The Vinegar Man is a long time dead: he died when he tore his valentine.

. . .

She, At His Funeral

THOMAS HARDY

They bear him to his resting-place—
  In slow procession sweeping by;
I follow at a stranger's space;
  His kindred they, his sweetheart I.
Unchanged my gown of garish dye,
  Though sable-sad is their attire;
But they stand round with griefless eye,
  Whilst my regret consumes like fire!

.   .   .

"The grave my little cottage is"

EMILY DICKINSON

The grave my little cottage is,
  Where, keeping house for thee,
I make my parlor orderly,
  And lay the marble tea,

For two divided, briefly,
  A cycle, it may be,
Till everlasting life unite
  In strong society.

.   .   .

I Shall Not Care

SARA TEASDALE

When I am dead and over me bright April
  Shakes out her rain-drenched hair,
Though you should lean above me broken-hearted,
  I shall not care.
I shall have peace, as leafy trees are peaceful
  When rain bends down the bough;
And I shall be more silent and cold-hearted
  Than you are now.

• • •

When Thou Must Home to Shades of Underground

THOMAS CAMPION

When thou must home to shades of underground,
And there arriv'd, a new admired guest,
The beauteous spirits do engirt thee round,
White Iope, blithe Helen, and the rest,
To hear the stories of thy finish'd love
From that smooth tongue whose music hell can move;

Then wilt thou speak of banqueting delights,
Of masques and revels which sweet youth did make,
Of tourneys and great challenges of knights,
And all these triumphs for thy beauty's sake:
When thou hast told these honours done to thee,
Then tell, O tell, how thou didst murder me.

• • •

"Over I journey" (from *Hymns to the Night*)

NOVALIS

Over I journey
And for each pain
A pleasant sting only
Shall one day remain.
Yet in a few moments
Then free am I,
And intoxicated
In Love's lap lie.
Life everlasting
Lifts, wave-like, at me,
I gaze from its summit
Down after thee.
Your lustre must vanish
Yon mound underneath —
A shadow will bring thee
Thy cooling wreath.
Oh draw at my heart, love,
Draw till I'm gone,
That, fallen asleep, I
Still may love on.
I feel the flow of
Death's youth-giving flood
To balsam and ether
Transform my blood —
I live all the daytime
In faith and in might
And in holy fire
I die every night.

Translated from the German by George MacDonald

• • •

Over the Coffin

THOMAS HARDY

They stand confronting, the coffin between,
His wife of old, and his wife of late,
And the dead man whose both they had been
Seems listening aloof, as to things past date.
—"I have called," says the first. "Do you marvel or not?"
"In truth," says the second, "I do—somewhat."
"Well, there was a word to be said by me! . . .
I divorced that man because of you—
It seemed I must do it, boundenly;
But now I am older, and tell you true,
For life is little, and dead lies he;
I would I had let alone you two!
And both of us, scorning parochial ways,
Had lived like the wives in the patriarchs' days."

• • •

She Weeps Over Rahoon

JAMES JOYCE

Rain on Rahoon falls softly, softly falling
Where my dark lover lies.
Sad is his voice that calls me, sadly calling
At grey moonrise.

Love, hear thou
How soft, how sad his voice is ever calling,
Ever unanswered, and the dark rain falling,
Then as now.

Dark too our hearts, O love, shall lie and cold
As his sad heart has lain
Under the moongrey nettles, the black mould
And muttering rain.

• • •

"She dwelt among the untrodden ways"

WILLIAM WORDSWORTH

She dwelt among the untrodden ways
Beside the springs of Dove,
A maid whom there were none to praise
And very few to love;

A violet by a mossy stone
Half hidden from the eye!
—Fair as a star when only one
Is shining in the sky.

She lived unknown, and few could know
When Lucy ceased to be;
But she is in her grave, and, oh,
The difference to me!

• • •

"Come not, when I am dead"

ALFRED, LORD TENNYSON

Come not, when I am dead,
  To drop thy foolish tears upon my grave,
To trample round my fallen head,
  And vex the unhappy dust thou wouldst not save.
There let the wind sweep and the plover cry;
      But thou, go by.

Child, if it were thine error or thy crime
  I care no longer, being all unblest:
Wed whom thou wilt, but I am sick of Time,
  And I desire to rest.
Pass on, weak heart, and leave me where I lie:
      Go by, go by.

• • •

Remember

CHRISTINA ROSSETTI

Remember me when I am gone away,
  Gone far away into the silent land;
  When you can no more hold me by the hand,
Nor I half turn to go yet turning stay.
Remember me when no more day by day
  You tell me of our future that you plann'd:
  Only remember me; you understand
It will be late to counsel then or pray.
Yet if you should forget me for a while
  And afterwards remember, do not grieve;
  For if the darkness and corruption leave
  A vestige of the thoughts that once I had,
Better by far you should forget and smile
  Than that you should remember and be sad.

• • •

"This living hand, now warm and capable"

JOHN KEATS

This living hand, now warm and capable
Of earnest grasping, would, if it were cold
And in the icy silence of the tomb,
So haunt thy days and chill thy dreaming nights
That thou wouldst wish thine own heart dry of blood
So in my veins red life might stream again,
And thou be conscience-calm'd—see here it is—
I hold it towards you.

• • •

From "The Triumph of Time"

ALGERNON CHARLES SWINBURNE

I wish we were dead together to-day,
    Lost sight of, hidden away out of sight,
Clasped and clothed in the cloven clay,
    Out of the world's way, out of the light,
Out of the ages of worldly weather,
Forgotten of all men altogether,
As the world's first dead, taken wholly away,
    Made one with death, filled full of the night.

How we should slumber, how we should sleep,
    Far in the dark with the dreams and the dews!
And dreaming, grow to each other, and weep,
    Laugh low, live softly, murmur and muse;
Yea, and it may be, struck through by the dream,
Feel the dust quicken and quiver, and seem
Alive as of old to the lips, and leap
    Spirit to spirit as lovers use.

Sick dreams and sad of a dull delight;
    For what shall it profit when men are dead
To have dreamed, to have loved with the whole soul's might,
    To have looked for day when the day was fled?
Let come what will, there is one thing worth,
To have had fair love in the life upon earth:
To have held love safe till the day grew night,
    While skies had colour and lips were red.

• • •

He Wishes His Beloved Were Dead

W.B. YEATS

Were you but lying cold and dead,
And lights were paling out of the West,
You would come hither, and bend your head,
And I would lay my head on your breast;
And you would murmur tender words,
Forgiving me, because you were dead:
Nor would you rise and hasten away,
Though you have the will of the wild birds,
But know your hair was bound and wound
About the stars and moon and sun:
O would, beloved, that you lay
Under the dock-leaves in the ground,
While lights were paling one by one.

• • •

Sonnets from the Portugese XXIII

ELIZABETH BARRETT BROWNING

Is it indeed so? If I lay here dead,
    Wouldst thou miss any life in losing mine?
    And would the sun for thee more coldly shine
    Because of grave-damps falling round my head?
    I marvelled, my Belovëd, when I read
    Thy thought so in the letter. I am thine,
    But . . . so much to thee? Can I pour thy wine
    While my hands tremble? Then my soul, instead
    Of dreams of death, resumes life's lower range.
    Then, love me, Love! look on me, breathe on me!
    As brighter ladies do not count it strange,
    For love, to give up acres and degree,
    I yield the grave for thy sake, and exchange
    My near sweet view of heaven, for earth with thee!

• • •

she lived

after he died
what really happened is
she watched the days
bundle into thousands,
watched every act become
the history of others,
every bed more
narrow,
but even as the eyes of lovers
strained toward the milky young
she walked away
from the hole in the ground
deciding to live.   and she lived.

. . .

You Bring Out the Dead in Me

RITA MAE REESE

Not the living dead but the dead dead: the righteous dead
who have waited for the pale horse so they can stop being
so dead. You call forth the callused fingers of Johnny Cash
softened during June-less weeks to my deadened
surface. Everywhere, my skin is whirlpools of fingertips
regaining sensation, waiting. You bring out all of the
dead white men in me—entire anthologies of them, my spine
cracking like a loose canon. Whitman & multitudes of dead
or dying soldiers, Keats & Fanny, Hopkins & God all crowd
up inside me, electric wires writhing. You rewind me to
the moment the dead first began to outnumber the living, when
Lazarus returned to tip the scales back, to stave off the inevitable.
In the invisible cities of the dead, I walk star-lined streets,
multiplied beyond endurance. You have resurrected the
Rita Hayworth in me, the Mae West. And we all rise up, as good as dead.

. . .

Apparent Death

JOHANN WOLFGANG VON GOETHE

Weep, maiden, weep here o'er the tomb of Love;

He died of nothing—by mere chance was slain.
But is he really dead?—oh, that I cannot prove:

A nothing, a mere chance, oft gives him life again.

Translated from the German by Edward Alfred Bowring

the four-legged and the winged

In which the poets remind us that everything that lives, dies

The Dead Sparrow

CATULLUS

Ye Cupids droop each little head,
Nor let your wings with joy be spread,
My Lesbia's favourite bird is dead,
Which dearer than her eyes she lov'd:
For he was gentle and so true,
Obedient to her call he flew,
No fear, no wild alarm he knew,
But lightly o'er her bosom mov'd.

And softly fluttering here, and there,
He never sought to cleave the air,
But chirrup'd oft, and free from care,
Tun'd to her ear his grateful strain.
But now he's pass'd the gloomy bourn,
From whence he never can return,
His death, and Lesbia's grief I mourn,
Who sighs alas! but sighs in vain.

Oh curst be thou! devouring grave!
Whose jaws eternal victims crave,
From whom no earthly power can save,
For thou hast ta'en the bird away.
From thee, my Lesbia's eyes o'erflow,
Her swollen cheeks with weeping glow,
Thou art the cause of all her woe,
Receptacle of life's decay.

Translated from the Latin by Lord Byron

• • •

Epitaph to a Dog

LORD BYRON

Near this Spot
are deposited the Remains of one
who possessed Beauty without Vanity,
Strength without Insolence,
Courage without Ferosity,
and all the virtues of Man without his Vices.

This praise, which would be unmeaning Flattery
if inscribed over human Ashes,
is but a just tribute to the Memory of
BOATSWAIN, a DOG,
who was born in Newfoundland May 1803
and died at Newstead Nov. 18, 1808.

When some proud Son of Man returns to Earth,
Unknown by Glory, but upheld by Birth,
The sculptor's art exhausts the pomp of woe,
And storied urns record who rests below.
When all is done, upon the Tomb is seen,
Not what he was, but what he should have been.
But the poor Dog, in life the firmest friend,
The first to welcome, foremost to defend,
Whose honest heart is still his Master's own,
Who labours, fights, lives, breathes for him alone,
Unhonoured falls, unnoticed all his worth,
Denied in heaven the Soul he held on earth —
While man, vain insect! hopes to be forgiven,
And claims himself a sole exclusive heaven.

Oh man! thou feeble tenant of an hour,
Debased by slavery, or corrupt by power—
Who knows thee well must quit thee with disgust,
Degraded mass of animated dust!
Thy love is lust, thy friendship all a cheat,
Thy tongue hypocrisy, thy heart deceit!

By nature vile, ennobled but by name,
Each kindred brute might bid thee blush for shame.
Ye, who perchance behold this simple urn,
Pass on—it honors none you wish to mourn.
To mark a friend's remains these stones arise;
I never knew but one—and here he lies.

• • •

North Beach Chinese Sonnet

BARRY GIFFORD

Chinese children chase pigeons
    fish swirl
    in ponds
at evening—

I think
of my four-day dead cat
that was such a beauty,
all black with a touch
of white on her belly—

Nothing is more unbelievable
than death, —
I keep looking around
for what's
not there.

• • •

Funeral Oration for a Mouse

ALAN DUGAN

This, Lord, was an anxious brother and
a living diagram of fear: full of health himself,
        he brought diseases like a gift
to give his hosts. Masked in a cat's moustache
        but sounding like a bird, he was a ghost
            of lesser noises and a kitchen pest
for whom some ladies stand on chairs. So,
Lord, accept our felt though minor guilt
        for an ignoble foe and ancient sin:
            the murder of a guest
        who shared our board: just once he ate
            too slowly, dying in our trap
from necessary hunger and a broken back.

Humors of love aside, the mousetrap was our own
        opinion of the mouse, but for the mouse
            it was the tree of knowledge with
            its consequential fruit, the true cross
        and the gate of hell. Even to approach
            it makes him like or better than
its maker: his courage as a spoiler never once
impressed us, but to go out cautiously at night
        into the dining room—what bravery, what
            hunger! Younger by far, in dying he
was older than us all: his mobile tail and nose
spasmed in the pinch of our annoyance. Why,
then, at that snapping sound, did we, victorious,
            begin to laugh without delight?

        Our stomachs, deep in an analysis
            of their own stolen baits
(and asking, "Lord, Host, to whom are we the pests?"),
        contracted and demanded a retreat
        from our machine and its effect of death,
            as if the mouse's fingers, skinnier

than hairpins and as breakable as cheese,
could grasp our grasping lives, and in
their drowning movement pull us under too,
into the common death beyond the mousetrap.

· · ·

Traveling through the Dark

WILLIAM STAFFORD

Traveling through the dark I found a deer
dead on the edge of the Wilson River road.
It is usually best to roll them into the canyon:
that road is narrow; to swerve might make more dead.

By glow of the tail-light I stumbled back of the car
and stood by the heap, a doe, a recent killing;
she had stiffened already, almost cold.
I dragged her off; she was large in the belly.

My fingers touching her side brought me the reason—
her side was warm; her fawn lay there waiting,
alive, still, never to be born.
Beside that mountain road I hesitated.

The car aimed ahead its lowered parking lights;
under the hood purred the steady engine.
I stood in the glare of the warm exhaust turning red;
around our group I could hear the wilderness listen.

I thought hard for us all—my only swerving—,
then pushed her over the edge into the river.

· · ·

Fox

LINDA HOGAN

Every day he announces his presence, clockwork.
I see the fox, the tail so full
and I want to touch it.
The face so sweet, the white muzzle,
the way it moves from one side of the hill to another,
memorizing every stone,
the way it lies down on ground to watch me,
as if it is easy and not just fear, not hunger.
And when I see it
I have to love it and hate it
because its body is my cat,
my neighbor's cat,
and even though I hurt
I know that this was not a gunshot,
not an accident on the road,
not a long illness.
This is god swallowing what it must.

•   •   •

White Rat

LUCIA PERILLO

Etherized in a bell jar, they resembled tiny sandbags, stacked

We carried each by its tail, their feet like newborn grappling hooks

Their insides had vaginal qualities, pink and wet and gleaming

The tissue hummed

My scalpel got jittery

I sewed up my rat as soon as I could

Because I realized the spiderwebstuff holding us here is thin

It was in fact difficult to account for all the people walking around not
   dead

I don't think I ever cut the gland I was supposed to, out

In the coming weeks, in lab-light, I made up little prayers-slash-songs

Like: *Please white rat*

Let me not have damaged you

You to whom I will be shackled all my years

You out of all your million brethren

If not genetically identical, then close

My rat went back to its Tupperware basin

With the cedar chips and the drinking bottle

That went *chingle chingle* whenever water was sipped

Which reassured me, knowing my rat was staying well hydrated

Though most of them languished

Which was, after all, their purpose

Though my rat stayed fat

Suggesting I'd botched the job of excising its adrenal

Not that its fatness saved it in the end

When all the living ones were gassed

Because the Christmas break had nearly come

Because of the deadline for the postmortem dissection

And time for the final roundup of facts

Oh rat

As you snuffle through your next incarnation

Say as my albino postman

Or my Japanese neurologist who taps her mallet on my knee

While I try not to visualize myself with your pink eyes and flaky scalp

Your scabrous tail especially

Because I have killed plenty of other things

But none of them have claimed me the way you did

• • •

Upon Butchering of the Hog

SAMANTHA COLE

There is a golden time
to warn of endings
when ridge runners herd
sows from lots.
Hooks in hooves,
chain over bough.
Men of dirt drawing-up
their harvest towards the sun.

Watch and learn,
Sisters:
Struggle will ruin the meat.
The shot must be clean.

. . .

Earth Cafeteria

LINH DINH

Mudman in earth cafeteria,
I eat aardwolf. I eat ant bear.
I eat mimosa, platypus, ermine.

"White meat is tasteless, dark meat stinks."
(The other white meat is pork, triple X.)

Rice people vs. bread people.
White bread vs. wheat bread.
White rice vs. brown rice.
Manhattan vs. New England.
Kosher sub-gum vs. knuckle kabob.

"What is patriotism but love of the foods one had as a child?"*

To eat stinky food
is a sign of savagery, humility,
identification with the earth.

"It was believed that after cleaning, tripe still contained ten percent
excrement which was therefore eaten with the rest of the meal."**

Today I'll eat Colby cheese.
Tomorrow I'll eat sparrows.
Chew bones, suck fat,
bite heads off, gnaw on a broken wing.

Anise-flavored beef soup smells like sweat.
A large sweaty head bent over
a large bowl of sweat soup.

A Pekinese is ideal, will feed six,
but an unscrupulous butcher
will fudge a German shepherd,
chopping it up to look like a Pekinese.

Toothless man sucking
a pureed porterhouse steak
with a straw.

Parboiled placenta.

To skewer and burn meat is barbaric.
To boil, requiring a vessel, is a step up.
To microwave.

People who eat phalli, hot dogs, kielbasas
vs. people who eat balls.

To eat with a three-pronged spear and a knife.
To eat with two wooden sticks.
To eat with the hands.

Boiling vs. broiling.

To snack on a tub of roasted grasshoppers at the movies.

*Lin Yutang
**Mikhail Bakhtin

•　•　•

haiku

FRED WEINER

hind end destroyed
thrashing in the roadside ditch—
yearling fawn

. . .

Affinity: Mustang

LINDA HOGAN

Tonight after the sounds of day
have given way
she stands beneath the moon,
a gray rock shining.
She matches the land,
belonging.

She has a dark calm face,
her hooves like black stone
belong to the earth
the way it used to be,
long grasses
as grass followed rain
or wind laid down the plains of fall
or in winter now when
her fur changes and becomes snow
or her belly hair turns the color of red water willows
at the creek,
her legs black as trees.

These horses
almost a shadow,
broken.
When we walk together
in the tall grasses, I feel her

as if I am walking with mystery,
with beauty and fierce powers,
as if for a while we are the same animal
and remember each other from before.

Or sometimes I sit on earth
and watch the wind blow her mane and tail
and the waves of dry grasses
all one way
and it calls to mind
how I've come such a long way
through time
to find her.

Some days I sing to her
remembering the Kiowa man
who sang to cover the screams
of their ponies killed by the Americans,
songs I know in my sleep.

Some nights, hearing her outside,
I think she is to the earth
what I am to her,
belonging.

Last night it was her infant that died
after the kinship and movement
of so many months.
Tonight I sit on straw
and watch milk stream from her nipples
to the ground. I clean her face.
I've come such a long way through time
to find her and
it is the first time
I have ever seen a horse cry.

Sing then, the wind says,
Sing.

• • •

Some Heaven

TODD DAVIS

The rabbit's head is caught
between the slats of the fence,
and in its struggle it has turned
so the hind legs nearly touch
the nose—neck broken, lungs failing.
My boys ask me to do something
but see no mercy in my plan.
At five and eight, they are so far
away from their own deaths
that they cannot imagine the blessing
a shovel might hold, the lesson
suffering offers those who have
not suffered.

At bedtime, my youngest prays
the rabbit is in a heaven
where there are no fences, where
there is more than enough to eat.
He begins to cry and we rock
until sleep's embrace takes him
from me. I know his prayer is right.
What more should heaven be?
A place wild with carrot and dill,
sunflower and phlox, fields
that stretch on for miles, every coyote
full, every hawk passing over, a warm
October day that need never end.

• • •

Something Fragile, Broken

PAULA GUNN ALLEN

1.
i had seen something
i had wanted

and sorrow is not to enter
into it:

a sparrow falling: a tiny
fragile egg, crushed

it was in the grass then
fallen, dead.

reached out, that hand,
palm open, such care

fallen anyway, all the way
to the ground

where it smashed.
the slate stones that ringed

the lily pond of my grandmother
held it, blue and broken.

sorrow was not to enter
into it, but it did.

and i am not stone but shell,
blue and fragile, dropped,

i splatter, spill the light
all over the stone

nothing that can be mended.

2.
sorrow was not to enter into this

but it did. and i
was not to weep, or

think such things or
let you see that this,

which was not to be entered,
was born and broken before

entering. not in tears
exactly, not fallen in

that way, but still
and i knew what would not

be spoken. a circle that
would not be broken

shattered anyway, or died.
like ripples on the lake,

when the stone has sunk
deep beneath the surface,

die. sorrow has no part
in it. some things just

don't go on. some circles
come undone. some sparrows

fall. sometimes sorrow
in spite of resolution,

enters in.

.   .   .

For Jan, With Love

DAVID LEE

1.

John he comes to my house
pulls his beat up truck in my drive
and honks
Dave John sez Dave my red sow
she got pigs stuck and my big hands they wont go
and I gotta get them pigs out
or that fucker shes gonna die
and I sez John goddam
well be right down and John sez Jan
he yells JAN wheres Jan shes got little hands
she can get in there and pull them pigs
and I sez Jan and he sez Jan and Jan comes
what? Jan sez and John sez tell Jan Dave
and I sez Jan Johns red sows got pigs
stuck and his hands too big and wont go
and hes gotta get them pigs out
or that fuckers gonna die (John he turns
his head and lights a cigarette)
(he dont say fuck to no woman)
and Jan she sez well lets go
and we get in Johns beat up damn truck
and go to pull Johns pigs

2.

Johns red sow she doesn't weigh
a hundred and sixty pounds
but he bred her to his biggest boar
and had to put hay bales by her sides
so the boar wouldn't break
her back because Carl bet five dollars
he couldnt and John he bet
five she could and John he won
but Carl enjoyed watching anyway

163

3.

Johns red sow was laying
on her side hurting bad
and we could see she had a pig
right there but it wouldnt come she
was too small and John sez see
and I sez I see that pigs gotta come out
or that fuckers gonna die
and Jan puts vaseline on her hands
and sez hold her legs and I hold her legs
and Jan goes in after the pig
and John gets out of the pen and goes
somewheres else

Jan she pulls like hell pretty soon
the pig come big damn big little pig
dead and I give Jan more vaseline and she goes
back to see about any more
and Johns red sow pushes hard on Jans arm
up to her elbow inside and Jan sez
theres more help me and I help
another pig damn big damn dead comes
and Johns red sow she seems better
and we hope thats all

4.

Johns red sow wont go
out of labor so we stay all night
and John brings coffee and smokes
and flashlight batteries and finally Jan
can feel another pig but Johns red sows
swole up tight and she cant grab hold
but only touch so I push her side
and she grunts and screams and shits all over Jans arm
and Jan sez I got it help me and I help
and we pull for a goddam hour and pull
the pigs head off

and I sez oh my god we gotta get that pig now
or that fuckers gonna die for sure
and John sez what happened? and Jan
gives him a baby pigs head in his hand
and John goes somewheres else again
while Jan goes back fast inside
grabbing hard and Johns red sow
hurts bad and Jan sez I got something help me
and I help and we start taking that pig out
piece by piece.

5.

Goddamn you bitch dont you die
Jan yells when Johns red sow dont help no more
and we work and the sun comes up
and we finally get the last piece of pig out
and give johns red sow a big shot of penicillin
her ass swole up like a football
but she dont labor and John sez
is that all? and Jan wipes her bloody arms
on a rag and sez yes and John climbs in
the pen and sez hows my red sow?
and we look and go home and go to bed
because Johns red sow that fucker she died

• • •

Rock Paper Scissors

MIRANDA BEESON

Carol's just back from Chappaquiddick where they sell
jars of oil for drowning ticks at the corner store.
A local boy showed her where the Kopechne girl died.
She thought it would be a mansion by a lake
but it was just an old shack by a brackish pond.
The boy said Mary Jo was pregnant, I say Rose
made him do it like Mother at the Bates Motel.

When I was little my brother and I had different
ways of killing a tick, all of them horrible.
Sometimes we'd skit it back and forth,
using two wood matches for sticks,
crouched on the warm tar road in front of the hedge
back from the beach, salty and bored.
Then we would set it on fire.
I would tell myself later in my prim twin bed,
under the dark roar of August's cicadas
that he made me do it, but knew it wasn't true.
Knew the stock-still second of orange ignition
made my skin prick alive.

· · ·

Song

BRIGIT PEGEEN KELLY

Listen: there was a goat's head hanging by ropes in a tree.
All night it hung there and sang. And those who heard it
Felt a hurt in their hearts and thought they were hearing
The song of a night bird. They sat up in their beds, and then
They lay back down again. In the night wind, the goat's head
Swayed back and forth, and from far off it shone faintly,
The way the moonlight shone on the train track miles away
Beside which the goat's headless body lay. Some boys
Had hacked its head off. It was harder work than they had imagined.
The goat cried like a man and struggled hard. But they
Finished the job. They hung the bleeding head by the school
And then ran off into the darkness that seems to hide everything.
The head hung in the tree. The body lay by the tracks.
The head called to the body. The body to the head.
They missed each other. The missing grew large between them,
Until it pulled the heart right out of the body, until
The drawn heart flew toward the head, flew as a bird flies
Back to its cage and the familiar perch from which it trills.
Then the heart sang in the head, softly at first and then louder,

Sang long and low until the morning light came up over
The school and over the tree, and then the singing stopped. . . .
The goat had belonged to a small girl. She named
The goat Broken Thorn Sweet Blackberry, named it after
The night's bush of stars, because the goat's silky hair
Was dark as well water, because it had eyes like wild fruit.
The girl lived near a high railroad track. At night
She heard the trains passing, the sweet sound of the train's horn
Pouring softly over her bed, and each morning she woke
To give the bleating goat his pail of warm milk. She sang
Him songs about girls with ropes and cooks in boats.
She brushed him with a stiff brush. She dreamed daily
That he grew bigger, and he did. She thought her dreaming
Made it so. But one night the girl didn't hear the train's horn.
And the next morning she woke to an empty yard. The goat
Was gone. Everything looked strange. It was as if a storm
Had passed through while she slept, wind and stones, rain
Stripping the branches of fruit. She knew that someone
Had stolen the goat and that he had come to harm. She called
To him. All morning and into the afternoon, she called
And called. She walked and walked. In her chest a bad feeling
Like the feeling of stones gouging the soft undersides
Of her bare feet. Then somebody found the goat's body
By the high tracks, the flies already filling their soft bottles
At the goat's torn neck. Then somebody found the head
Hanging in a tree by the school. They hurried to take
These things away so that the girl would not see them.
They hurried to raise money to buy the girl another goat.
They hurried to find the boys who had done this, to hear
Them say it was a joke, a joke, it was nothing but a joke. . . .
But listen: here is the point. The boys thought to have
Their fun and be done with it. It was harder work than they
Had imagined, this silly sacrifice, but they finished the job,
Whistling as they washed their large hands in the dark.
What they didn't know was that the goat's head was already
Singing behind them in the tree. What they didn't know
Was that the goat's head would go on singing, just for them,
Long after the ropes were down, and that they would learn to listen,

Pail after pail, stroke after patient stroke. They would
Wake in the night thinking they heard the wind in the trees
Or a night bird, but their hearts beating harder. There
Would be a whistle, a hum, a high murmur, and, at last, a song,
The low song a lost boy sings remembering his mother's call.
Not a cruel song, no, no, not cruel at all. This song
Is sweet. It is sweet. The heart dies of this sweetness.

violence

In which the poets shows us the reality of war and murder,
disasters and terrorism

Do Not Weep, Maiden, For War Is Kind

STEPHEN CRANE

Do not weep, maiden, for war is kind.
Because your lover threw wild hands toward the sky
And the affrighted steed ran on alone,
Do not weep.
War is kind.

Hoarse, booming drums of the regiment,
Little souls who thirst for fight,
These men were born to drill and die.
The unexplained glory flies above them,
Great is the battle-god, great, and his kingdom —
A field where a thousand corpses lie.

Do not weep, babe, for war is kind.
Because your father tumbled in the yellow trenches,
Raged at his breast, gulped and died,
Do not weep.
War is kind.

Swift blazing flag of the regiment,
Eagle with crest of red and gold,
These men were born to drill and die.
Point for them the virtue of slaughter,
Make plain to them the excellence of killing
And a field where a thousand corpses lie.

Mother whose heart hung humble as a button
On the bright splendid shroud of your son,
Do not weep.
War is kind.

• • •

The Man He Killed

THOMAS HARDY

"Had he and I but met
    By some old ancient inn,
We should have sat us down to wet
    Right many a nipperkin!

"But ranged as infantry,
    And staring face to face,
I shot at him as he at me,
    And killed him in his place.

"I shot him dead because—
    Because he was my foe,
Just so: my foe of course he was;
    That's clear enough; although

"He thought he'd 'list, perhaps,
    Off-hand like—just as I—
Was out of work—had sold his traps—
    No other reason why.

"Yes; quaint and curious war is!
    You shoot a fellow down
You'd treat if met where any bar is,
    Or help to half-a-crown."

• • •

Anthem for Doomed Youth

WILFRED OWEN

What passing-bells for these who die as cattle?
   Only the monstrous anger of the guns.
   Only the stuttering rifles' rapid rattle
Can patter out their hasty orisons.
No mockeries now for them; no prayers nor bells,
Nor any voice of mourning save the choirs,
The shrill, demented choirs of wailing shells;
And bugles calling for them from sad shires.

What candles may be held to speed them all?
   Not in the hands of boys, but in their eyes
Shall shine the holy glimmers of goodbyes.
   The pallor of girls' brows shall be their pall;
Their flowers the tenderness of patient minds,
And each slow dusk a drawing-down of blinds.

• • •

Dulce et Decorum Est

WILFRED OWEN

Bent double, like old beggars under sacks,
Knock-kneed, coughing like hags, we cursed through sludge,
Till on the haunting flares we turned our backs,
And towards our distant rest began to trudge.
Men marched asleep. Many had lost their boots,
But limped on, blood-shod. All went lame, all blind;
Drunk with fatigue; deaf even to the hoots
Of gas-shells dropping softly behind.

Gas! GAS! Quick, boys!—An ecstasy of fumbling
Fitting the clumsy helmets just in time,
But someone still was yelling out and stumbling
And flound'ring like a man in fire or lime.—

Dim through the misty panes and thick green light,
As under a green sea, I saw him drowning.

In all my dreams before my helpless sight
He plunges at me, guttering, choking, drowning.

If in some smothering dreams, you too could pace
Behind the wagon that we flung him in,
And watch the white eyes writhing in his face,
His hanging face, like a devil's sick of sin,
If you could hear, at every jolt, the blood
Come gargling from the froth-corrupted lungs
Obscene as cancer, bitter as the cud
Of vile, incurable sores on innocent tongues,—
My friend, you would not tell with such high zest
To children ardent for some desperate glory,
The old Lie: *Dulce et decorum est*
Pro patria mori.

• • •

Suicide in the Trenches

SIEGFRIED SASSOON

I knew a simple soldier boy
Who grinned at life in empty joy,
Slept soundly through the lonesome dark,
And whistled early with the lark.
In winter trenches, cowed and glum,
With crumps and lice and lack of rum,
He put a bullet through his brain.
No one spoke of him again.

You smug-faced crowds with kindling eye
Who cheer when soldier lads march by,
Sneak home and pray you'll never know
The hell where youth and laughter go.

• • •

In Flanders Fields

JOHN MCCRAE

In Flanders fields the poppies blow
   Between the crosses, row on row,
   That mark our place; and in the sky
   The larks, still bravely singing, fly
Scarce heard amid the guns below.

We are the Dead. Short days ago
We lived, felt dawn, saw sunset glow,
   Loved and were loved, and now we lie
      In Flanders fields.

Take up our quarrel with the foe:
To you from failing hands we throw
   The torch; be yours to hold it high.
   If ye break faith with us who die
We shall not sleep, though poppies grow
      In Flanders fields.

• • •

Back

WILFRED GIBSON

They ask me where I've been,
And what I've done and seen.
But what can I reply
Who know it wasn't I,
But someone just like me,
Who went across the sea
And with my head and hands
Killed men in foreign lands . . .
Though I must bear the blame
Because he bore my name.

• • •

From *Epitaphs of the War*

RUDYARD KIPLING

If any question why we died,
Tell them, because our fathers lied.

. . .

An Irish Airman Foresees His Death

W.B. YEATS

I know that I shall meet my fate
Somewhere among the clouds above;
Those that I fight I do not hate,
Those that I guard I do not love;
My country is Kiltartan Cross,
My countrymen Kiltartan's poor,
No likely end could bring them loss
Or leave them happier than before.
Nor law, nor duty bade me fight,
Nor public man, nor cheering crowds,
A lonely impulse of delight
Drove to this tumult in the clouds;
I balance all, brought all to mind,
The years to come seemed waste of breath,
A waste of breath the years behind
In balance with this life, this death.

. . .

The Dying Airman

WWI-ERA BRITISH MILITARY FOLKSONG

A handsome young airman lay dying,
    And as on the aerodrome he lay,
To the mechanics who round him came sighing,
    These last dying words he did say:
"Take the cylinders out of my kidneys,
    The connecting-rod out of my brain,
Take the cam box out of my backbone,
    And assemble the engine again."

• • •

From "Hugh Selwyn Mauberley"

EZRA POUND

These fought, in any case,
and some believing,
              pro domo, in any case . . .

Some quick to arm,
some for adventure,
some from fear of weakness,
some from fear of censure,
some for love of slaughter, in imagination,
learning later . . .
some in fear, learning love of slaughter;

Died some, pro patria,
            non "dulce" non "et decor" . . .
walked eye-deep in hell
believing in old men's lies, then unbelieving
came home, home to a lie,
home to many deceits,
home to old lies and new infamy;
usury age-old and age-thick
and liars in public places.

Daring as never before, wastage as never before.
Young blood and high blood,
Fair cheeks, and fine bodies;

fortitude as never before

frankness as never before,
disillusions as never told in the old days,
hysterias, trench confessions,
laughter out of dead bellies.

V
There died a myriad,
And of the best, among them,
For an old bitch gone in the teeth,
For a botched civilization,

Charm, smiling at the good mouth,
Quick eyes gone under earth's lid,

For two gross of broken statues,
For a few thousand battered books.

• • •

History's Juju

CAROL LEVIN

In 1944 Edward Teller pressed the button
on the Trinity bomb knowing
the atmosphere could

catch fire
The fire could circle and end the earth.
Teller pressed it
and waited.

• • •

The Second Slaughter

LUCIA PERILLO

Achilles slays the man who slayed his friend, pierces the corpse
behind the heels and drags it
behind his chariot like the cans that trail
a bride and groom. Then he lays out
a banquet for his men, oxen and goats
and pigs and sheep; the soldiers eat
until a greasy moonbeam lights their beards.

The first slaughter is for victory, but the second slaughter is for grief—
in the morning more animals must be killed
for burning with the body of the friend. But Achilles finds
no consolation in the hiss and crackle of their fat;
not even heaving four stallions on the pyre
can lift the ballast of his sorrow.

And here I turn my back on the epic hero—the one who slits
the throats of his friend's dogs,
killing what the loved one loved
to reverse the polarity of grief. Let him repent
by vanishing from my concern
after he throws the dogs onto the fire.
The singed fur makes the air too difficult to breathe.

When the oil wells of Persia burned I did not weep
until I heard about the birds, the long-legged ones especially
which I imagined to be scarlet, with crests like egrets
and tails like peacocks, covered in tar
weighting the feathers they dragged through black shallows
at the rim of the marsh. But once

I told this to a man who said I was inhuman, for giving animals
my first lament. So now I guard
my inhumanity like the jackal
who appears behind the army base at dusk,
come there for scraps with his head lowered

in a posture that looks like appeasement
though it is not.

.   .   .

So I Was a Coffin

GERARDO MENA

—For Corporal Kyle Powell, died in my arms, 04 November 2006

They said *you are a spear*. So I was a spear.

I walked around Iraq upright and tall, but the wind blew and I began to lean. I leaned into a man, who leaned into a child, who leaned into a city. I walked back to them and neatly presented a city of bodies packaged in rows. They said *no. You are a bad spear.*

They said *you are a flag*. So I was a flag.

I climbed to the highest building, in the city that had no bodies, and I smiled and waved as hard as I could. I waved too hard and I caught fire and I burned down the city, but it had no bodies. They said *no. You are a bad flag.*

They said *you are a bandage*. So I was a bandage.

I jumped on Kyle's chest and wrapped my lace arms together around his torso and pressed my head to his ribcage and listened to his heartbeat. Then I was full, so I let go and wrung myself out.

And I jumped on Kyle's chest and wrapped my lace arms together around his torso and pressed my head to his ribcage and listened to his heartbeat. Then I was full, so I let go and wrung myself out.

And I jumped on Kyle's chest and wrapped my lace arms together around his torso and pressed my head to his ribcage but there was no heartbeat. They said *no. You are a bad bandage.*

They said *you are a coffin*. So I was.

I found a man. They said he died bravely, or he will. I encompassed him
in my finished wood, and I shut my lid around us. As they lowered us
into the ground he made no sound because he had no eyes
and could not cry. As I buried us in dirt we held our breaths together
and they said, *yes. You are a good coffin.*

. . .

On the Russian Persecution of the Jews

ALGERNON CHARLES SWINBURNE

O son of man, by lying tongues adored,
By slaughterous hands of slaves with feet red-shod
  In carnage deep as Christian ever trod
Profaned with prayer and sacrifice abhorred
And incense from the trembling tyrant's horde,
  Brute worshippers or wielders of the rod,
  Most murderous even of all that call thee God,
Most treacherous even that ever called thee Lord;
Face loved of little children long ago,
Head hated of the priests and rulers then,
  If thou see this, or hear these hounds of thine
  Run ravening as the Gadarean swine,
Say, was not this thy Passion, to foreknow
  In death's worst hour the works of Christian men?

. . .

The Lynching

CLAUDE MCKAY

His spirit in smoke ascended to high heaven.
His father, by the cruelest way of pain,
Had bidden him to his bosom once again;
The awful sin remained still unforgiven.
All night a bright and solitary star
(Perchance the one that ever guided him,
Yet gave him up at last to Fate's wild whim)
Hung pitifully o'er the swinging char.
Day dawned, and soon the mixed crowds came to view
The ghastly body swaying in the sun:
The women thronged to look, but never a one
Showed sorrow in her eyes of steely blue;
And little lads, lynchers that were to be,
Danced round the dreadful thing in fiendish glee.

• • •

From "The Ballad of Reading Gaol"

OSCAR WILDE

He walked amongst the Trial Men
  In a suit of shabby grey;
A cricket cap was on his head,
  And his step seemed light and gay;
But I never saw a man who looked
  So wistfully at the day.

I never saw a man who looked
  With such a wistful eye
Upon that little tent of blue
  Which prisoners call the sky,
And at every drifting cloud that went
  With sails of silver by.

I walked, with other souls in pain,
  Within another ring,
And was wondering if the man had done
  A great or little thing,
When a voice behind me whispered low,
  "That fellow's got to swing."

Dear Christ! the very prison walls
  Suddenly seemed to reel,
And the sky above my head became
  Like a casque of scorching steel;
And, though I was a soul in pain,
  My pain I could not feel.

I only knew what hunted thought
  Quickened his step, and why
He looked upon the garish day
  With such a wistful eye;
The man had killed the thing he loved
  And so he had to die.

Yet each man kills the thing he loves
  By each let this be heard,
Some do it with a bitter look,
  Some with a flattering word,
The coward does it with a kiss,
  The brave man with a sword!

Some kill their love when they are young,
  And some when they are old;
Some strangle with the hands of Lust,
  Some with the hands of Gold:
The kindest use a knife, because
  The dead so soon grow cold.

Some love too little, some too long,
  Some sell, and others buy;
Some do the deed with many tears,
  And some without a sigh:

For each man kills the thing he loves,
  Yet each man does not die.

. . .

From *Eugene Onegin,* Canto Six: "The Duel"

ALEXANDER PUSHKIN

XXVII
The shining pistols are uncased,
The mallet loud the ramrod strikes,
Bullets are down the barrels pressed,
For the first time the hammer clicks.
Lo! poured in a thin gray cascade,
The powder in the pan is laid,
The sharp flint, screwed securely on,
Is cocked once more. Uneasy grown,
Guillot behind a pollard stood;
Aside the foes their mantles threw,
Zaretski paces thirty-two
Measured with great exactitude.
At each extreme one takes his stand,
A loaded pistol in his hand.

XXVIII
"Advance!"—
          Indifferent and sedate,
The foes, as yet not taking aim,
With measured step and even gait
Athwart the snow four paces came—
Four deadly paces do they span;
Oneguine slowly then began
To raise his pistol to his eye,
Though he advanced unceasingly.
And lo! five paces more they pass,
And Lenski, closing his left eye,
Took aim—but as immediately

Oneguine fired—Alas! alas!
The poet's hour hath sounded—See!
He drops his pistol silently.

. . .

Stagolee

US FOLK BALLAD

I got up one mornin' jes' 'bout four o'clock;
Stagolee an' big bully done have one finish' fight:
What 'bout? All 'bout dat raw-hide Stetson hat.

Stagolee shot Bully; Bully fell down on de flo',
Bully cry out: "Dat fohty-fo' hurts me so."
Stagolee done killed dat Bully now.

Sent for de wagon, wagon didn't come,
Loaded down wid pistols an' all dat gatlin' gun,
Stagolee done kill dat Bully now.

Some giv' a nickel, some giv' a dime,
I didn't give a red copper cent, 'cause he's no friend o' mine,
Stagolee done kill dat Bully now.

Carried po' Bully to cemetary, people standin' 'round,
When preacher say Amen, lay po' body down,
Stagolee done kill dat Bully now.

Fohty dollah coffin, eighty dollah hack,
Carried po' man to cemetery but failed to bring him back,
Ev'y body been dodgin' Stagolee.

. . .

Road Kill

KIMIKO HAHN

No one thought anything amiss
in the child's collection of road kill,

which in later years transformed
into the odd stash in the young man's sealed foot-locker

and a stolen store mannequin, and later still,
various South Asian boys abducted for experiments.

One Vietnamese boy in particular
fled naked and screaming into the street

but the police returned him to Jeffrey Dahmer
who apologized,

Sorry, officers, we had too much to drink—
Clearly a gay-thing, they figured, best to leave alone.

Yes, left alone—until a stench from his apartment

overwhelmed the poor Milwaukee neighborhood
and the investigation revealed

three male torsos in a tub of acid, rotting body parts,
a refrigerator of organs, complete skeletons,

and tools such as a Polaroid camera and drill—
I wanted to make them into zombies.

I didn't know how to make them stay—

Stay hand. Stay heart.
Stay still.

• • •

Juárez

LUCIA PERILLO

At night the bones move where the animals take them,
bones of the girls that once were girls,
the hand-bones missing, you know how it goes,
you fill in the blank, the unimaginable X
of horrid futures. From bus stops
before dawn, from outside the maquiladoras
when the horizon bites the sun's gold coin,
from the hundred places to fail to arrive at
or return from, the bones uncouple
their linkages and travel separate ways.
Too many of them for just one theory—
too many skulls for the drug lords even,
for the husbands the satanists the cross-border whore-killers
 . . . until you start to suspect the dirt itself.
Between the concrete wall and the drainage ditch,
the sheet-metal scraps and the collapsed storm fence,
a desert of ocotillo scrub, not even one decent
cowboy cactus, one bent arm
swearing an oath of truth. When I was younger
I wrote this poem many times and don't know
where I was going with it: so much worship
for every speck of mica giving off
a beam I made into a blade. And you can see
how I turned mere rocks into villains
when it turns out the landscape's not at fault,
the parched land a red herring—this is not the song
of how the men fried while hiding inside the boxcar
(and even then someone outside locked the door).
My poems took place where the wind-skids sang:
perhaps I've been too fond of railroad tracks
and the weedy troughs alongside them, which do
accept most everything. Especially the spikes,
how I loved those spikes cast into silence,
in this case behind the factories, where the grass

grows sparser than in the poor soils of Texas,
a place with completely different ghosts
lying just over the river. To get there
you will have to pass by a large pink cross
made out of such spikes at the border station,
and here's the main thing, forgive me, I missed in my youth:
how from each spike hangs a name.

•   •   •

Homicide Detective

KATHLEEN SHEEDER BONANNO

In the morning
we rush up to him
where he stands
in Leidy's misbegotten little yard
looking at the dirt.
I think, *Is this*
what gathering clues looks like?

But his is the voice of water.
Only he knows the right words to say,
and he says them:
I promise we will get this guy.

When I show him a photo
he says, *She's beautiful;*
almost how she looked
when we found her.

And now I know who to believe.
What does the coroner, who says
she had maggots in her mouth,
know about the truth?

•   •   •

South Central Los Angeles Death Trip, 1982

WANDA COLEMAN

1
jes another X marking it

dangling gold chains & pinky rings
nineteen. done in black leather & defiance
teeth white as halogen lamps, skin dark as a threat
they spotted him taking in the night
made for the roust
arrested him on suspicion of
they say he became violent
they say he became combative in the rear seat of
that sleek zebra maria. they say
it took a chokehold to restrain him
and then they say he died of asphyxiation
on the spot

summarized in the coroner's report
as the demise of
one more nondescript dustbunny
ripped on phencyclidine
(which justified their need to
leave his hands cuffed behind his back
long after rigor mortis set in)

2
stress had damaged his thirty-nine-year-old mind
more than he could admit but he was trying
to make life work as well as it could
for a father with three children praying
dad will pull through

where the butcher knife came from
no one's sure. they say
he held off ten riot squad patrol cars
for forty-five minutes outside that 109th street

church. they say the cops had stopped him
because they didn't like his looks.
they say something fragile inside his head
snapped. they say it took twenty rounds of ammo
to bring him down they say he took five
gunshot pellets & thirteen bullets
they say that was a lot of outrage over
a case of misconstrued identity

3
she was fed up that day with
everything. now here they come turning off
the damned gas so she went and
chased the service rep
from the yard before he could carry out the
disconnection order. by the time
police officers arrived she had lost what was
left of her common sense
had grabbed up & brandished an eleven-inch
boning knife to back up her mouth.
the two officers complained she threw
that knife at them. and they were so terrified
they didn't consider a wounding. they
simply emptied both guns
into the thirty-nine-year-old hefty female.
it took twelve shots to
subdue all that treataniggahthis
and whitesonofabitchesthat,
they said, and killed it

4
strangely he was dodging & ducking,
    bouncing & rolling,
    tipping & slipping
(as if dangling from the end of it)
in and out of traffic in front of the sheriff's
station, embarrassing them, causing a modest jam
    for no apparent reason

189

therefore they arrested the twenty-six-year-old
descendant of slaves and booked him for
this queer behavior, their spokesman said
        because there weren't
enough terrorists, assassins or irate taxpayers
to keep them busy that Wednesday afternoon.
        he was handcuffed
and left alone in his cell and fell inexplicably
into unconsciousness in a mere three hours,
        they said. he was
rushed to a nearby hospital still in cuffs
where he died within twenty-two minutes.

cause of demise as unknown as ever

5
without evidence to support the supposition
they swore the twenty-one-year-old
consumer was involved in the robbery of
the popular Manchester Avenue chicken shack,
and not just another hungry-but-innocent bystander
he was assumed guilty, if not the brainiac
perhaps the getaway driver. he was captured during
the fray before questions could be asked or
players & slayers identified. that he was unarmed
was not a pertinent issue. that he was ignorant
decidedly was. they handcuffed him and made
him lay on the ground in the middle of the fray
where, unfortunately, his ignorance got
him killed by police gunfire. they say an officer
yelled freeze and this inexperienced
young black hoodlum being unfamiliar with the
procedure of how one freezes while being held face down
on the sidewalk, hands cuffed behind one's back
could not do so. therefore the inability to freeze
under these conditions cost him his life

6
exhausted after working the nightshift
he was so dead on his feet he couldn't
hear 'em ramming in his door, so they broke into
the sepia-toned man's apartment by mistake
(it was supposed to be the one downstairs).
officers swarmed his bed as he opened his eyes.
officers were on him like maggots on foul meat.
nevertheless he managed to free himself long
enough to run into the bathroom where
he was ultimately subdued without ever knowing why

the coroner reported this
as death due to heart attack
brought on by advanced arteriosclerosis
in a twenty-eight-year-old black male

7
he was bound for college but was caught
standing on a street corner blocks from home
maybe, like they say, he had recently scored some
dope (which could not be found) or maybe
minutes earlier he'd been snaking on that
ham sandwich mama made for her nineteen-year-old
sure is handsome fine young black man.
maybe there was nothing to it at all, not even
that missing piece of aluminum foil the officers
claim they saw him pull out of his trousers

sudden-like

as they happened to be cruising past. it made
a mysterious metallic gleam
which they mistook for the glint of steel
which is why there was all that draw-and-fire
which is why

mama went to his funeral instead of his graduation

8

all of twenty-six, the ebony diabetic had
no steady job and lived with his parents.
he was a young man with mental & physical
problems. He began to act strangely, they say
although no one noticed him brandishing
that piece of radiator fan belt or that
kitchen knife in the middle of the street.
perhaps some car somewhere had broken down
certainly, he had, enough to make the sheriff's
deputies approach with caution and order him
to freeze, he turned toward them and even
though he was fourteen feet away from them his
turning toward them inspired so much fear
in the armed men one of them emptied his
Smith & Wesson service revolver into the
young diabetic who died from three slugs

9

that night Bob came blamming on her door.
she had just gotten home from working
the register at the club and her feet were
killing her, now here come some numbskull
sayhisnameis Bob knocking the damn door
in with some okey-doke about "here come da
police, hide me quick!" so she got something
for Bob's jive probably-drunk ass, that .22
caliber rifle she uses regularly to scare off
the riffraff, then she cracked the door a taste
but before she could make her melodrama move
it slammed open and she was blinded by the
flash as she took a shot in her left breast.
the bullet entered her right rib cage and killed
the 8 ½-month old baby she was carrying.
all this behind a supposedtobe drug bust where
no drugs were found by the officers in charge

jes another X marking it

• • •

Killers

CARL SANDBURG

I am put high over all others in the city today.

I am the killer who kills for those who wish a killing today.

Here is a strong young man who killed.
There was a driving wind of city dust and horse dung blowing and he
stood at an intersection of five sewers and there pumped the bullets of an
automatic pistol into another man, a fellow citizen.

Therefore, the prosecuting attorneys, fellow citizens, and a jury of his
peers, also fellow citizens, listened to the testimony of other fellow
citizens, policemen, doctors, and after a verdict of guilty, the judge, a
fellow citizen, said: I sentence you to be hanged by the neck till you are
dead.

So there is a killer to be killed and I am the killer of the killer for today.
I don't know why it beats in my head in the lines I read once in an old
school reader: I'm to be queen of the May, mother, I'm to be queen
of the May.
Anyhow it comes back in language just like that today.

I am the high honorable killer today.
There are five million people in the state, five million killers for
whom I kill
I am the killer who kills today for five million killers who wish a killing.

• • •

Dropping the Lamb

RICHARD M. BERLIN

> *If you're alone in the kitchen and drop the lamb, you can always just*
> *pick it up. Who's going to know it?*
> —Julia Child

Imagine a neurosurgeon in scrubs
hunched over a dead man's chart

writing loops and strands
of twisted prose

illegible as pasta
lying on a plate.

Imagine the quick snip of day-old sutures,
scalpel slicing a crust of blood,

the careful retraction of scalp and brain
to retrieve a wad of gauze

left behind like yesterday's paper
on the back seat of a bus.

And imagine the patient's brainstem
herniating through the foramen magnum

in less time than it takes a lamb
to drop from counter to floor,

how suddenly the heart stops beating,
nothing left for a neurosurgeon to write

except a post-op note
to erase responsibility

the way Julia would wipe
lamb's blood off the kitchen floor.

• • •

crepuscular (the family tomb)

ANDREI CODRESCU

bodies in the flood
just like in the days of noah
cemeteries rising
the dead are coming back
but no saints are marching in
Is that my body in the flood
no cause I'm not poor and black
stubborn crazy or sentimental
but it sure looks like the dead are coming back
it sure looks like a bad moon rising
bodies in the flood
just like in the days of noah
with nobody to pick them up
just like in the days of FEMA

• • •

Monongah, 1907

RITA MAE REESE

In the worst mining accident in US history, the coal company hid the
truth by reducing the number killed by nearly 200 men and boys.

Goods were thrown from the shelves
of the company store,
the river reached for
the railroad tracks, the hill

lunged away from itself.
The houses on the hill
lifted and shook. The bank,
not yet finished,

trembled but its beams held.

Later, the newspapers
printed rumors of incredible
escapes: men shot

straight through air holes,
whole as ever,
and twice as alive. Children
gathered around

the entrances. Women tore
at their hair
and scratched their faces.
The dead were taken

out as they had gone in,
in twos and threes,
and carried to the bank like
something still valuable

and, like something once valuable,
they disappeared
as the counting began.

• • •

In the Free World

RUTH STONE

The teenager in for involvement
in murder and dismemberment
feels unjustly treated. He says,
"Why I never even got my driver's
license." He refers to his offense
as "catching his case." He feels
no remorse for burying the skinned
and beheaded female victim.

A short time ago it was only thirty,
but now for under a hundred dollars,
you can get a license enabling you
to legally sell weapons; handguns,
machine guns, you are an automatic
licensed dealer in automatics.

And the Mexican government,
after betraying the native Mexican
farmers, sends helicopters in
to bomb them and quell dissatisfaction.
It's quicker and maybe more humane
than just starving them. After
the insurrection, the dead Indians
lying in their own blood were found
to be carrying carved wooden guns,
just pieces of carved wood.

· · ·

Woman Martyr

AGI MISHOL

> *"The evening goes blind, and you are*
> *Only twenty."*
> —Nathan Alterman, Late Afternoon in the Market

You are only twenty
and your first pregnancy is a bomb.
Under your broad skirt you are pregnant with dynamite
and metal shavings. This is how you walk in the market,
ticking among the people, you, Andaleeb Takatka.

Someone loosened the screws in your head
and launched you toward the city;
even though you come from Bethlehem,
the Home of Bread, you chose a bakery.

And there you pulled the trigger out of yourself,
and together with the Sabbath loaves,
sesame and poppy seed,
you flung yourself into the sky.

Together with Rebecca Fink you flew up
with Yelena Konre'ev from the Caucasus
and Nissim Cohen from Afghanistan
and Suhila Houshy from Iran
and two Chinese you swept along
to death.

Since then, other matters
have obscured your story,
about which I speak all the time
without having anything to say.

Translated from the Hebrew by Lisa Katz

. . .

Flight

MIRANDA BEESON

An iridescent exhausted finch
found its way to your home
in the aftermath.
Trapped between screen and pane
you palmed him, brought him in,
built him a cage that was not a cage.
A hidden perch for the nights.
An aviary filled with light and seed
for the days.
Where had he come from?
A pet store in the shadow of the towers?
A tiny door unlatched by the blasts?
We pondered dark scenarios.

The survival of this speck
of feathered perfection seemed
more important than anything else
we could think of those first few weeks:
more important than the planes,
the slow motion tumble,
the man in his business suit
who fell through the air without
benefit of wings.

. . .

Fire and Ice

ROBERT FROST

Some say the world will end in fire,
Some say in ice.
From what I've tasted of desire
I hold with those who favor fire.
But if it had to perish twice,
I think I know enough of hate
To say that for destruction ice
Is also great
And would suffice.

facing one's demise

In which the poets deal with the inevitable

"Do not go gentle into that good night"

DYLAN THOMAS

Do not go gentle into that good night,
Old age should burn and rave at close of day;
Rage, rage against the dying of the light.

Though wise men at their end know dark is right,
Because their words had forked no lightning they
Do not go gentle into that good night.

Good men, the last wave by, crying how bright
Their frail deeds might have danced in a green bay,
Rage, rage against the dying of the light.

Wild men who caught and sang the sun in flight,
And learn, too late, they grieved it on its way,
Do not go gentle into that good night.

Grave men, near death, who see with blinding sight
Blind eyes could blaze like meteors and be gay,
Rage, rage against the dying of the light.

And you, my father, there on the sad height,
Curse, bless, me now with your fierce tears, I pray,
Do not go gentle into that good night.
Rage, rage against the dying of the light.

• • •

To Death

ANNE, COUNTESS OF WINCHILSEA

O King of Terrors, whose unbounded sway
All that have life, must certainly obey,
The King, the Priest, the Prophet, all are thine,
Nor wou'd ev'n God (in flesh) thy stroke decline.
My name is on thy roll, and sure I must
Increase thy gloomy kingdom in the dust.
My soul at this no apprehension feels,
But trembles at thy swords, thy racks, thy wheels;
Thy scorching fevers, which distract the sense,
And snatch us raving, unprepar'd from hence;
At thy contagious darts, that wound the heads
Of weeping friends, who wait at dying beds.
Spare these, and let thy time be when it will;
My bus'ness is to die, and thine to kill.
Gently thy fatal scepter on me lay,
And take to thy cold arms, insensibly, thy prey.

• • •

From *Julius Caesar*

WILLIAM SHAKESPEARE

Cowards die many times before their deaths.
The valiant never taste of death but once.
Of all the wonders that I yet have heard,
It seems to me most strange that men should fear,
Seeing that death, a necessary end,
Will come when it will come.

• • •

Learning a Word While Climbing

WILLIAM STAFFORD

Once I fell, already falling, and from that fall
lurched faster when I thought, "Oh, my guide,
now I know what came to you, the vision
your eyes told us you saw when you died!"

It was a clarity come upon
the mountains greater than the snow, a name
pronounced among them like an opening
when a traveler finds a pass and escapes a storm.

While I was falling I saw such light: saved,
my nylon rope came true and swung me free,
I hung above the world and saw it, never
so bright again, one long glimpse—*Eternity*.

•   •   •

Staying Under

RITA MAE REESE

In the shallow end   of the public swimming pool,
I stood unseen   behind my two older sisters,
my head just above water.   They counted to three and
we all went under. My eyes closed against the chlorine
I pictured the sun   on its surface, their faces
when I won. When I reached out to see if they were there
          my hands touched nothing. Then with both hands
               I held my breath down
until I couldn't feel   it matter.

My mother remembers the lifeguard bulleting into the pool
   & how her body felt like the gun that fired him, hard and still.

She remembers a blue daughter coming out of the water,
    CPR & vomiting. My sisters remember a girl dumb enough
to drown herself in three feet of water. I remember becoming
    the blue between sky and water.

. . .

A Contemplation upon Flowers

HENRY KING, BISHOP OF CHICHESTER

Brave flowers—that I could gallant it like you,
And be as little vain!
You come abroad, and make a harmless show,
And to your beds of earth again.
You are not proud: you know your birth:
For your embroider'd garments are from earth.
You do obey your months and times, but I
Would have it ever Spring:
My fate would know no Winter, never die,
Nor think of such a thing.
O that I could my bed of earth but view
And smile, and look as cheerfully as you!

O teach me to see Death and not to fear,
But rather to take truce!
How often have I seen you at a bier,
And there look fresh and spruce!
You fragrant flowers! then teach me, that my breath
Like yours may sweeten and perfume my death.

. . .

On the Brink of Death

MICHELANGELO

Now hath my life across a stormy sea
Like a frail bark reached that wide port where all
Are bidden, ere the final reckoning fall
Of good and evil for eternity.
Now know I well how that fond phantasy
Which made my soul the worshiper and thrall
Of earthly art, is vain; how criminal
Is that which all men seek unwillingly.
Those amorous thoughts which were so lightly dressed,
What are they when the double death is nigh?
The one I know for sure, the other dread.
Painting nor sculpture now can lull to rest
My soul that turns to His great love on high,
Whose arms to clasp us on the cross were spread.

Translated from the Italian by John Addington Symondas

• • •

"If I should die to-night"

ARABELLA E. SMITH

If I should die to-night,
My friends would look upon my quiet face
Before they laid it in its resting-place,
And deem that death had left it almost fair;
And, laying snow-white flowers against my hair,
Would smooth it down with tearful tenderness,
And fold my hands with lingering caress,—
Poor hands, so empty and so cold to-night!

If I should die to-night,
My friends would call to mind, with loving thought,
Some kindly deed the icy hands had wrought;

Some gentle word the frozen lips had said;
Errands on which the willing feet had sped.
The memory of my selfishness and pride,
My hasty words, would all be put aside,
And so I should be loved and mourned to-night.

If I should die to-night,
Even hearts estranged would turn once more to me,
Recalling other days remorsefully;
The eyes that chill me with averted glance
Would look upon me as of yore, perchance,
And soften in the old familiar way;
For who could war with dumb unconscious clay?
So I might rest, forgiven of all, to-night.

Oh, friends, I pray to-night
Keep not your kisses for my dead, cold brow—
The way is lonely, let me feel them now.
Think gently of me; I am travel-worn;
My faltering feet are pierced with many a thorn.
Forgive, oh, hearts estranged, forgive, I plead!
When dreamless rest is mine I shall not need
The tenderness for which I long to-night.

• • •

"Come away, come away, death" (from *Twelfth Night*)

WILLIAM SHAKESPEARE

Come away, come away, death,
And in sad cypress let me be laid.
Fly away, fly away, breath;
I am slain by a fair cruel maid.
　　My shroud of white, stuck all with yew, O prepare it!
　　My part of death, no one so true did share it.

Not a flower, not a flower sweet,
On my black coffin let there be strown.
Not a friend, not a friend greet
My poor corpse, where my bones shall be thrown.
    A thousand thousand sighs to save, lay me, O, where
    Sad true lover never find my grave, to weep there.

• • •

From "Ode to a Nightingale"

JOHN KEATS

Darkling I listen; and, for many a time
    I have been half in love with easeful Death,
Call'd him soft names in many a mused rhyme,
    To take into the air my quiet breath;
      Now more than ever seems it rich to die,
    To cease upon the midnight with no pain,
      While thou art pouring forth thy soul abroad
        In such an ecstasy!
    Still wouldst thou sing, and I have ears in vain—
      To thy high requiem become a sod.

• • •

"In Love With Easeful Death"

MARY E. FLETCHER

"In love with easeful death?" Not I,
Too well I love this friendly sky,
The sunrise and the sunset hour,
The winter storm and summer shower,
The hand-clasp and the glad surprise
Of welcome in a good friend's eyes.

In truth, I have a secret dread
Of lying down among the dead,

The poor, white dead bereft of will,
Who lie so cold, so strangely still,
The while we break our hearts and pray
For one fond word of yesterday.

I'd go as children do, at night,
When they must leave the warmth and light,
With lagging step and looks behind
At toys beloved and faces kind,
Only half sure of God to keep
Strange terrors from them while they sleep.

• • •

To One Shortly to Die

WALT WHITMAN

From all the rest I single out you, having a message for you,
You are to die—let others tell you what they please, I cannot prevaricate,
I am exact and merciless, but I love you—there is no escape for you.

Softly I lay my right hand upon you, you 'ust feel it,
I do not argue, I bend my head close and half envelop it,
I sit quietly by, I remain faithful,
I am more than nurse, more than parent or neighbor,
I absolve you from all except yourself spiritual bodily, that is
eternal, you yourself will surely escape,
The corpse you will leave will be but excrementitious.

The sun bursts through in unlooked-for directions,
Strong thoughts fill you and confidence, you smile,
You forget you are sick, as I forget you are sick,
You do not see the medicines, you do not mind the weeping friends,
I am with you,
I exclude others from you, there is nothing to be commiserated,
I do not commiserate, I congratulate you.

• • •

Finish

CARL SANDBURG

Death comes once, let it be easy.
Ring one bell for me once, let it go at that.
Or ring no bell at all, better yet.

Sing one song if I die.
Sing John Brown's Body or Shout All Over God's Heaven.
Or sing nothing at all, better yet.

Death comes once, let it be easy.

. . .

Sleep, Darksome, Deep

PAUL VERLAINE

Sleep, darksome, deep,
    Doth on me fall:
  Vain hopes all, sleep,
    Sleep, yearnings all!

  Lo, I grow blind!
    Lo, right and wrong
Fade to my mind . . .
    O sorry song!

  A cradle, I,
    Rocked in a grave:
Speak low, pass by,
    Silence I crave!

Translated from the French by Gertrude Hall

. . .

Finis

E.E. CUMMINGS

Over silent waters
                                  day descending
                                                      night ascending
floods the gentle glory of the sunset
In a golden greeting
                                        splendidly to westward
as pale twilight
                  trem-
                          bles
                                    into
                                              Darkness
comes the last light's gracious exhortation
                                                      Lifting up to peace
so when life shall falter
                                      standing on the shores of the
eternal
god
      May I behold my sunset
Flooding
      over silent waters

· · ·

From "Graveyard by the Sea"

PAUL VALÉRY

Even as a fruit's absorbed in the enjoying,
Even as within the mouth its body dying
Changes into delight through dissolution,
So to my melted soul the heavens declare
All bounds transfigured into a boundless air,
And I breathe now my future's emanation.

Translated from the French by C. Day Lewis

· · ·

Laughter and Death

WILFRID SCAWEN BLUNT

There is no laughter in the natural world
Of beast or fish or bird, though no sad doubt
Of their futurity to them unfurled
Has dared to check the mirth-compelling shout.
The lion roars his solemn thunder out
To the sleeping woods. The eagle screams her cry.
Even the lark must strain a serious throat
To hurl his blest defiance at the sky.
Fear, anger, jealousy, have found a voice.
Love's pain or rapture the brute bosoms swell.
Nature has symbols for her nobler joys,
Her nobler sorrows. Who had dared foretell
That only man, by some sad mockery,
Should learn to laugh who learns that he must die?

· · ·

A Ballad of Suicide

G.K. CHESTERSON

The gallows in my garden, people say,
Is new and neat and adequately tall;
I tie the noose on in a knowing way
As one that knots his necktie for a ball;
But just as all the neighbours—on the wall—
Are drawing a long breath to shout "Hurray!"
The strangest whim has seized me. . . . After all
I think I will not hang myself to-day.

To-morrow is the time I get my pay—
My uncle's sword is hanging in the hall—
I see a little cloud all pink and grey—
Perhaps the rector's mother will not call—

I fancy that I heard from Mr. Gall
That mushrooms could be cooked another way—
I never read the works of Juvenal—
I think I will not hang myself to-day.

The world will have another washing-day;
The decadents decay; the pedants pall;
And H.G. Wells has found that children play,
And Bernard Shaw discovered that they squall,
Rationalists are growing rational—
And through thick woods one finds a stream astray
So secret that the very sky seems small—
I think I will not hang myself to-day.

ENVOI

Prince, I can hear the trumpet of Germinal,
The tumbrils toiling up the terrible way;
Even to-day your royal head may fall,
I think I will not hang myself to-day.

．　．　．

From "Of the Last Verses in the Book"

EDMUND WALLER

The soul's dark cottage, batter'd and decay'd,
Lets in new light through chinks that time has made;
Stronger by weakness, wiser men become
As they draw near to their eternal home:
Leaving the old, both worlds at once they view,
That stand upon the threshold of the new.

．　．　．

Fear

SARA TEASDALE

I am afraid, oh I am so afraid!
The cold black fear is clutching me to-night
As long ago when they would take the light
And leave the little child who would have prayed,
Frozen and sleepless at the thought of death.
My heart that beats too fast will rest too soon;
I shall not know if it be night or noon,—
Yet shall I struggle in the dark for breath?
Will no one fight the Terror for my sake,
The heavy darkness that no dawn will break?
How can they leave me in that dark alone,
Who loved the joy of light and warmth so much,
And thrilled so with the sense of sound and touch,—
How can they shut me underneath a stone?

• • •

From *Measure for Measure*

WILLIAM SHAKESPEARE

If I must die,
I will encounter darkness as a bride,
And hug it in mine arms.

• • •

"So proud she was to die"

EMILY DICKINSON

So proud she was to die
It made us all ashamed
That what we cherished, so unknown
To her desire seemed.

So satisfied to go
Where none of us should be,
Immediately, that anguish stooped
Almost to jealousy.

. . .

From *Macbeth*

WILLIAM SHAKESPEARE

Duncan:
Is execution done on Cawdor?
Are not those in commission yet return'd?

Malcolm:
My liege, they are not yet come back.
But I have spoke with one that saw him die:
Who did report that very frankly
He confess'd his treasons, implored your Highness' pardon,
And set forth a deep repentance:
Nothing in his life became him
Like the leaving it.

. . .

Upon a Passing Bell

THOMAS WASHBOURNE

Hark, how the Passing Bell
Rings out thy neighbour's knell!
    And thou, for want of wit
    Or grace, ne'er think'st on it;
Because thou yet art well!

Fool! In two days, or three,
The same may ring for thee!

For Death's impartial dart
  Will surely hit thy heart!
He will not take a fee!

Since, then, he will not spare,
See thou thyself prepare
  Against that dreadful day,
  When thou shalt turn to clay!
This Bell bids thee, Beware!

. . .

When I Have Fears That I May Cease to Be

JOHN KEATS

When I have fears that I may cease to be
  Before my pen has gleaned my teeming brain,
Before high-pilèd books, in charactery,
  Hold like rich garners the full ripened grain;
When I behold, upon the night's starred face,
  Huge cloudy symbols of a high romance,
And think that I may never live to trace
  Their shadows with the magic hand of chance;
And when I feel, fair creature of an hour,
  That I shall never look upon thee more,
Never have relish in the faery power
  Of unreflecting love—then on the shore
Of the wide world I stand alone, and think
Till love and fame to nothingness do sink.

. . .

From "Good-bye"

RALPH WALDO EMERSON

Good-bye, proud world! I'm going home:
Thou art not my friend, and I'm not thine.
Long through thy weary crowds I roam;
A river-ark on the ocean brine,
Long I've been tossed like the driven foam;
But now, proud world! I'm going home.

Good-bye to Flattery's fawning face;
To Grandeur with his wise grimace;
To upstart Wealth's averted eye;
To supple Office, low and high;
To crowded halls, to court and street;
To frozen hearts and hasting feet;
To those who go, and those who come;
Good-bye, proud world! I'm going home.

• • •

Elegy

CHIDIOCK TICHBORNE

My prime of youth is but a frost of cares,
My feast of joy is but a dish of pain,
My crop of corn is but a field of tares,
And all my good is but vain hope of gain;
    The day is past, and yet I saw no sun,
    And now I live, and now my life is done.

My tale was heard and yet it was not told,
My fruit is fallen, and yet my leaves are green,
My youth is spent and yet I am not old,
I saw the world and yet I was not seen;
    My thread is cut and yet it is not spun,
    And now I live, and now my life is done.

I sought my death and found it in my womb,
I looked for life and saw it was a shade,
I trod the earth and knew it was my tomb,
And now I die, and now I was but made;
  My glass is full, and now my glass is run,
  And now I live, and now my life is done.

· · ·

The Quatrain

FRANÇOIS VILLON

Made by Villon when he was sentenced to death

For my sorrow, I am François,
Born in Paris near to Pantoise.
Soon the six-foot cord that sways
Will teach my neck what my ass weighs.

· · ·

From "Growing Old"

LORD BYRON

What are the hopes of man? Old Egypt's King
  Cheops erected the first Pyramid
And largest, thinking it was just the thing
  To keep his memory whole, and mummy hid;
But somebody or other rummaging,
  Burglariously broke his coffin's lid:
Let not a monument give you or me hopes,
Since not a pinch of dust remains of Cheops.

But I, being fond of true philosophy,
    Say very often to myself, "Alas!
All things that have been born were born to die,
    And flesh (which Death mows down to hay) is grass;
You've passed your youth not so unpleasantly,
    And if you had it o'er again—'twould pass—
So thank your stars that matters are no worse,
And read your Bible, sir, and mind your purse."

   • • •

Death and the Unfortunate

JEAN DE LA FONTAINE

A poor unfortunate, from day to day,
Call'd Death to take him from this world away.
  "O Death," he said, "to me how fair thy form!
Come quick, and end for me life's cruel storm."
Death heard, and with a ghastly grin,
Knock'd at his door, and enter'd in.
"Take out this object from my sight!"
    The poor man loudly cried.
"Its dreadful looks I can't abide;
O stay him, stay him, let him come no nigher;
O Death! O Death! I pray thee to retire!"

    A gentleman of note
In Rome, Maecenas, somewhere wrote:—
"Make me the poorest wretch that begs,
Sore, hungry, crippled, clothed in rags,
In hopeless impotence of arms and legs;
    Provided, after all, you give
    The one sweet liberty to live:
I'll ask of Death no greater favour
Than just to stay away for ever."

Translated from the French by Elizur Wright

   • • •

"Since There Is No Escape"

SARA TEASDALE

Since there is no escape, since at the end
  My body will be utterly destroyed,
This hand I love as I have loved a friend,
  This body I tended, wept with and enjoyed;
Since there is no escape even for me
  Who love life with a love too sharp to bear:
The scent of orchards in the rain, the sea
  And hours alone too still and sure for prayer—
Since darkness waits for me, then all the more
Let me go down as waves sweep to the shore
  In pride; and let me sing with my last breath;
In these few hours of light I lift my head;
Life is my lover—I shall leave the dead
  If there is any way to baffle death.

the crossing

In which the poets chart the moment of death

"I heard a fly buzz when I died"

EMILY DICKINSON

I heard a fly buzz when I died;
  The stillness round my form
Was like the stillness in the air
  Between the heaves of storm.

The eyes beside had wrung them dry,
  And breaths were gathering sure
For that last onset, when the king
  Be witnessed in his power.

I willed my keepsakes, signed away
  What portion of me I
Could make assignable,—and then
  There interposed a fly,

With blue, uncertain, stumbling buzz,
  Between the light and me;
And then the windows failed, and then
  I could not see to see.

•   •   •

The Given

LINDA HOGAN

Some say our lives come from the wind.
The human, others say, is made by the mother of corn,
or clay given breath, a rib,
or comes from the great dreaming,
a congress of words and songs.

We walked out of the ocean, barely,
and gave ourselves to earth
and the ancients gave us our secret names
knowing, being human, we would forget them.

And yes, there was the one who carried a pitcher
full with the nectar of immortality
given only to the gods.
And the Chinese said there were 365 gods of the body
but to speak their names was to lose them.

I think of this, watching those who are walking today
into the river in garments of white, offering themselves,
their names, to save their souls.

Every day I ask myself, what is a human?
The present is so bare and tender
like the garments of the newly saved
I can see through, the revealed
nipple, thighs, buttocks
and I wonder which of the 365 gods
are inside the body today
and if in the future
when the air leaves your lungs
and, as some say, you stand at the beginning
of a tunnel,
you remember your name.
No, not that one, the real one,
The Given, the one
lost somewhere
along the way.

•   •   •

Prospice

ROBERT BROWNING

Fear death? — to feel the fog in my throat,
The mist in my face,
When the snows begin, and the blasts denote
I am nearing the place,
The power of the night, the press of the storm,
The post of the foe;
Where he stands, the Arch Fear in a visible form,
Yet the strong man must go:
For the journey is done and the summit attained,
And the barriers fall,
Though a battle's to fight ere the guerdon be gained,
The reward of it all.
I was ever a fighter, so — one fight more,
The best and the last!
I would hate that death bandaged my eyes, and forbore,
And bade me creep past.
No! let me taste the whole of it, fare like my peers
The heroes of old,
Bear the brunt, in a minute pay glad life's arrears
Of pain, darkness and cold.
For sudden the worst turns the best to the brave,
The black minute's at end,
And the elements' rage, the fiend-voices that rave,
Shall dwindle, shall blend,
Shall change, shall become first a peace out of pain,
Then a light, then thy breast,
O thou soul of my soul! I shall clasp thee again,
And with God be the rest!

• • •

Stars, Songs, Faces

CARL SANDBURG

Gather the stars if you wish it so.
Gather the songs and keep them.
Gather the faces of women.
Gather for keeping years and years.

  And then . . .
Loosen your hands, let go and say good-by.
  Let the stars and songs go.
  Let the faces and years go.
  Loosen your hands and say good-by.

• • •

The King of Thule

JOHANN WOLFGANG VON GOETHE

In Thule lived a monarch,

Still faithful to the grave,
To whom his dying mistress

A golden goblet gave.

Beyond all price he deem'd it,

He quaff'd it at each feast;
And, when he drain'd that goblet,

His tears to flow ne'er ceas'd.

And when he felt death near him,

His cities o'er he told,
And to his heir left all things,

But not that cup of gold.

A regal banquet held he

In his ancestral ball,
In yonder sea-wash'd castle,

'Mongst his great nobles all.

There stood the aged reveller,

And drank his last life's-glow,—
Then hurl'd the holy goblet

Into the flood below.

He saw it falling, filling,

And sinking 'neath the main,
His eyes then closed for ever,

He never drank again.

Translated from the German by Edward Alfred Bowring

• • •

dying

LUCILLE CLIFTON

i saw a small moon rise
from the breast of a woman
lying in a hospital hall
and I saw that the moon was me
and I saw that the punctured bag
of a woman body was me
and i saw you sad there in the lobby
waiting to visit and I wanted
to sing to you
go home
i am waiting for you there

• • •

Death at Daybreak

ANNE REEVE ALDRICH

I shall go out when the light comes in—
  There lie my cast-off form and face;
I shall pass Dawn on her way to earth,
  As I seek for a path through space.

I shall go out when the light comes in
  Would I might take one ray with me!
It is blackest night between the worlds,
  And how is a soul to see?

• • •

Upon His Departure Hence

ROBERT HERRICK

Thus I
Pass by,
And die:
As one
Unknown
And gone:
I'm made
A shade,
And laid
I' th' grave:
There have
My cave,
Where tell
I dwell.
Farewell.

· · ·

The Dying Man and the Vulture

KAHLIL GIBRAN

Wait, wait yet awhile, my eager friend.
I shall yield but too soon this wasted thing,
Whose agony overwrought and useless
Exhausts your patience.
I would not have your honest hunger
Wait upon these moments:
But this chain, though made of breath,
Is hard to break.
And the will to die,
Stronger than all things strong,
Is stayed by a will to live
Feebler than all things feeble.
Forgive me, comrade; I tarry too long.

It is memory that holds my spirit;
A procession of distant days,
A vision of youth spent in a dream,
A face that bids my eyelids not to sleep,
A voice that lingers in my ears,
A hand that touches my hand.
Forgive me that you have waited too long.
It is over now, and all is faded:
The face, the voice, the hand and the mist that brought them hither.
The knot is untied.
The cord is cleaved.
And that which is neither food nor drink is withdrawn.
Approach, my hungry comrade;
The board is made ready.
And the fare, frugal and spare,
Is given with love.
Come, and dig your beak here, into the left side,
And tear out of its cage this smaller bird,
Whose wings can beat no more:
I would have it soar with you into the sky.
Come now, my friend, I am your host tonight,
And you my welcome guest.

•   •   •

"I've seen a dying eye"

EMILY DICKINSON

I've seen a dying eye
Run round and round a room
In search of something, as it seemed,
Then cloudier become;
And then, obscure with fog,
And then be soldered down,
Without disclosing what it be,
'Twere blessed to have seen.

•   •   •

new orleans limbo

ANDREI CODRESCU

when it happens all of a sudden
it takes a while to realize you're dead
you keep eating that étoufée
wondering why it don't get any smaller
you keep talking to your friends
amused by their look of instant horror
you keep running that commercial
urging folks to make their reservations
come early and stay late
you keep posting all those deals
this is the best real estate
the best for all eternity
it takes a while to realize you're dead
this is eternity
when it happens just like that

· · ·

Being Born, Then Dying

ELIZABETH OAKES

When you become a body,
it tightens around
you with a sound like
insects in a haiku.

Then, this body loosens
like jeans you've worn
three times, and you will
slip out of it with no
more thought than that.

remains and rituals

In which the poets examine corpses, visit graveyards, attend funerals, and otherwise deal with physical remains

Common Dust

GEORGIA DOUGLAS JOHNSON

And who shall separate the dust
What later we shall be:
Whose keen discerning eye will scan
And solve the mystery?

The high, the low, the rich, the poor,
The black, the white, the red,
And all the chromatique between,
Of whom shall it be said:

Here lies the dust of Africa;
Here are the sons of Rome;
Here lies the one unlabelled,
The world at large his home!

Can one then separate the dust?
Will mankind lie apart,
When life has settled back again
The same as from the start?

. . .

The Sin-Eater

RITA MAE REESE

one hired to take upon himself the sins of a deceased person
by means of food eaten above the dead body (from the OED*)*

That first girl's name has long been forgotten
by everyone save me. She was young, fourteen or so,
and the daughter of a laborer. Then a carriage accident,
How shall I describe it? Her sins smacked of turnips and leeks.

How would innocence taste, I wonder. Pride is like
molded bread, abandoned cake, crumbs in a wood
that all the animals—even the birds—have fled. Save one.
Idolatry mushrooms in the mouth, adultery is a raw onion,

and hatred cooked cabbage—it is what I eat most often.
How do the living not gag on the smell? Will there be another
after me? I am old and full of ghosts. No one speaks to me
without there's been a death. But who needs words?

Most are lies anyway, tasting of pottage. People die,
you can count on them for it, God bless them.
Then over their bodies it's bread and porridge
I eat with clean fingers. I used to follow him,

the old sin-eater, asking him questions:
Was it always the same meal? Did it ever spill?
How much did he eat? Then one day he didn't answer my knock;
inside I found a fresh loaf of bread—three slices cut off—

and a bowl of gruel and him more silent than ever,
under a meal that was venial, mortal, and rotten.

• • •

Resurrection, or What He Told Me to Do When He Died

TODD DAVIS

Take me to the field where the river runs
by the swamp. Dig a hole deep enough
that dogs and coyotes won't dine on
what's left. Place cedar boughs
beneath my head, cover my body with ash
from the fireplace, dirt from the garden.
Spread seed here and there in no particular
pattern. Don't visit until warmth comes back
into the earth and spring rains move on. Then

see how jewelweed sprouts from my chest
and clover climbs from my eyes.

• • •

The Difference

EMILY FERRARA

I wrestled your ashes from the funeral urn,
a cylinder, too narrow at the neck. The plastic bag
held fine sand, a crumbled wall of ecru and pearl.
I tried to weigh you on the bathroom scale.
I held you, stepped on the scale, stepped off,
put you on the edge of the sink, stepped on again—
holding, not holding: the difference.
I didn't trust it. I took your ashes to the market,
placed the bag on the produce scale,
watched it sway. I bought three nectarines,
each one unblemished gold, and crimson.
Six-and-three-quarter pounds
you weighed, two pounds less than at birth.

• • •

Under the Vulture Tree

DAVID BOTTOMS

We have all seen them circling pastures,
have looked up from the mouth of a barn, a pine clearing,
the fences of our own backyards, and have stood
amazed by the one slow wing beat, the endless dihedral drift.
But I had never seen so many so close, hundreds,
every limb of the dead oak feathered black,

and I cut the engine, let the river grab the jon boat
and pull it toward the tree.
The black leaves shined, the pink fruit blossomed
red, ugly as a human heart.
Then, as I passed under their dream, I saw for the first time
its soft countenance, the raw fleshy jowls
wrinkled and generous, like the faces of the very old
who have grown to empathize with everything.

And I drifted away from them, slow, on the pull of the river,
reluctant, looking back at their roost,
calling them what I'd never called them, what they are,
those dwarfed transfiguring angels,
who flock to the side of the poisoned fox, the mud turtle
crushed on the shoulder of the road,
who pray over the leaf-graves of the anonymous lost,
with mercy enough to consume us all and give us wings.

. . .

June Night

SARA TEASDALE

Oh Earth, you are too dear to-night,
  How can I sleep while all around
Floats rainy fragrance and the far
  Deep voice of the ocean that talks to the ground?

Oh Earth, you gave me all I have,
  I love you, I love you,—oh what have I
That I can give you in return—
  Except my body after I die?

. . .

Statuary

NICK FLYNN

Bees may be trusted, always,
to discover the best, nay, the only

human, solution. Let me cite

an instance; an event, that,

though occurring in nature, is still
in itself wholly abnormal. I refer

to the manner in which the bees

will dispose of a mouse
or a slug

that may happen to have found its way
into the hive.

The intruder killed,

they have to deal with
the body,

which will very soon poison

their dwelling. If it be impossible

for them to expel or dismember it,
they will proceed methodically

& hermetically

to enclose it in a veritable sepulcher
of propolis & wax,

which will tower fantastically

above the ordinary monuments
of the city.

*

When we die
our bodies powder, our bodies

the vessel & the vessel
empties.

Our dying does not fill
the hive with the stench

of dying. But outside
the world hungers.

A cockroach, stung,
can be dragged back out.

A careless child

forced a snail inside with a stick once.
We waxed over the orifice of its shell

sealing the creature in. And here,

the bottom of the comb,
a mouse,
driven in by winter & lack.

Its pawing woke us. We stung it

dead.

Even before it died it reeked — worse
the moment it ceased
twitching.

Now everyday
we crawl over it
to pass outside,

the wax form of what was

staring out, its airless sleep,

the mouse we built
to warn the rest from us.

• • •

The Corpse

CHARLES BAUDELAIRE

Remember, my Beloved, what thing we met
By the roadside on that sweet summer day;
There on a grassy couch with pebbles set,
A loathsome body lay.

The wanton limbs stiff-stretched into the air,
Steaming with exhalations vile and dank,
In ruthless cynic fashion had laid bare
The swollen side and flank.

On this decay the sun shone hot from heaven
As though with chemic heat to broil and burn,
And unto Nature all that she had given
A hundredfold return.

The sky smiled down upon the horror there
As on a flower that opens to the day;
So awful an infection smote the air,
Almost you swooned away.

The swarming flies hummed on the putrid side,
Whence poured the maggots in a darkling stream,

That ran along these tatters of life's pride
With a liquescent gleam.

And like a wave the maggots rose and fell,
The murmuring flies swirled round in busy strife:
It seemed as though a vague breath came to swell
And multiply with life

The hideous corpse. From all this living world
A music as of wind and water ran,
Or as of grain in rhythmic motion swirled
By the swift winnower's fan.

And then the vague forms like a dream died out,
Or like some distant scene that slowly falls
Upon the artist's canvas, that with doubt
He only half recalls.

A homeless dog behind the boulders lay
And watched us both with angry eyes forlorn,
Waiting a chance to come and take away
The morsel she had torn.

And you, even you, will be like this drear thing,
A vile infection man may not endure;
Star that I yearn to! Sun that lights my spring!
O passionate and pure!

Yes, such will you be, Queen of every grace!
When the last sacramental words are said;
And beneath grass and flowers that lovely face
Moulders among the dead.

Then, O Beloved, whisper to the worm
That crawls up to devour you with a kiss,
That I still guard in memory the dear form
Of love that comes to this!

Translated from the French by James Huneker

• • •

The Corpse Washers

RAINER MARIA RILKE

They'd gotten used to him, until
the kitchen lamp was lit
to flicker in the eddies of that gloom;
but the unknown one stayed all unknown.

They washed his throat and neck,
and since they knew nothing of his life,
they made another for him,
as they kept on their washing.

One girl had to cough,
and set down the sponge,
vinegar-soaked, on his face.
Then the others paused—a moment's respite,
and from her scrub brush, the bristles dripped,
while his horrid hand . . . gnarled as if in cramp,
as if in protest: Tell them all,
he no longer thirsted.

It worked. They cleared their throats,
as one embarrassed and hurried up the work,
so that on the wall among the flowered patterns,
their shadows hunched and lurched,
as if taken in a net; they writhed in quiet,
until the washing ended.

The night, pressed against the bare window frame,
was pitiless, and the one without a name
lay stark and naked there,
and gave commands.

Translated from the German by Kent H. Dixon

• • •

From "Death Universal"

ROBERT BLAIR

What is this world?
What but a spacious burial-field unwall'd,
Strew'd with Death's spoils, the spoils of animals
Savage and tame, and full of dead men's bones!

The very turf on which we tread once liv'd;
And we that live must lend our carcases
To cover our own offspring: in their turns
They too must cover theirs. 'Tis here all meet!

. . .

From "The Indian Burying-Ground"

PHILIP FRENEAU

In spite of all the learned have said,
  I still my old opinion keep;
The posture that we give the dead
  Points out the soul's eternal sleep.

Not so the ancients of these lands;—
  The Indian, when from life released,
Again is seated with his friends,
  And shares again the joyous feast.

His imaged birds, and painted bowl,
  And venison, for a journey dressed,
Bespeak the nature of the soul,
  Activity, that wants no rest.

His bow for action ready bent,
  And arrows with a head of stone,
Can only mean that life is spent,
  And not the old ideas gone.

Thou, stranger, that shalt come this way,
  No fraud upon the dead commit,—
Observe the swelling turf, and say,
  They do not lie, but here they sit.

. . .

In a Burying Ground

SARA TEASDALE

This is the spot where I will lie
  When life has had enough of me,
These are the grasses that will blow
  Above me like a living sea.

These gay old lilies will not shrink
  To draw their life from death of mine,
And I will give my body's fire
  To make blue flowers on this vine.

"O Soul," I said, "have you no tears?
  Was not the body dear to you?"
I heard my soul say carelessly,
  "The myrtle flowers will grow more blue."

. . .

"them bones"

LUCILLE CLIFTON

them bones
them bones will
rise again
them bones
them bones will
walk again

them bones
them bones will
talk again
now hear
the word of The Lord
　　　　—Traditional

atlantic is a sea of bones,
my bones,
my elegant afrikans
connecting whydah and new york,
a bridge of ivory.

seabed they call it.
in its arms my early mothers sleep.
some women leapt with babies in their arms.
some women wept and threw babies in.

maternal armies pace the atlantic floor.
i call my name into the roar of surf
and something awful answers.

●　●　●

In the Cemetery

DAVID MORTON

I
I never come here but I see
　This same old woman, wearing years
That bear her head and shoulders down;
　Her eyes are dry of tears.

Each headstone has some tale for her,
　From each to each she goes.
They tell her things she understands
　About the folks she knows.

Now, living things are dumb and strange;
  She turns away her head.
I think she's more at home put here
  Among the speaking dead.

II
"Love of life," logicians say,
  "Inherent passion of the race;"
Yet here is what I found today
  Upon a woman's face:

Such longing as I have not seen
  Was in her thoughtful eyes,
That watched a double bed of green
  Where but one sleeper lies.

III
Grave-diggers are a cheerful lot:
  "Fine mornin', sir," he said.
I fancied that a murmur waked
  Among the listening dead.

"Fine mornin' up above," word passed
  From each to each below.
I'm glad the digger spoke out loud;
  I think they like to know.

. . .

Of Him I Love Day and Night

WALT WHITMAN

Of him I love day and night I dream'd I heard he was dead,
And I dream'd I went where they had buried him I love, but he was not
    in that place,
And I dream'd I wander'd searching among burial-places to find him,
And I found that every place was a burial-place;
The houses full of life were equally full of death, (this house is now,)

The streets, the shipping, the places of amusement, the Chicago, Boston,
   Philadelphia, the Mannahatta, were as full of the dead as of the living,
And fuller, O vastly fuller of the dead than of the living;
And what I dream'd I will henceforth tell to every person and age,
And I stand henceforth bound to what I dream'd,
And now I am willing to disregard burial-places and dispense with them,
And if the memorials of the dead were put up indifferently everywhere,
   even in the room where I eat or sleep, I should be satisfied,
And if the corpse of any one I love, or if my own corpse, be duly render'd
   to powder and pour'd in the sea, I shall be satisfied,
Or if it be distributed to the winds I shall be satisfied.

• • •

"Pia, Caritatevole, Amorosissima"

FRIEDRICH NIETZSCHE

Cave where the dead ones rest,
marble falsehood, thee
I love: for easy jest
My soul thou settest free.

To-day, to-day alone,
My soul to tears is stirred,
At thee, the pictured stone,
At thee, the graven word.

This picture (none need wis)
I kissed the other day.
When there's so much to kiss
Why did I kiss the—clay?

Who knows the reason why?
"A tombstone fool!" you laugh:
I kissed—I'll not deny—
E'en the long epitaph.

Translated from the German by Anthony M. Ludovici

• • •

Cemetery Chess

SANDY MCINTOSH

We lower my brother's coffin
beneath his monument.
Abruptly, mother hisses: "Look!"
Not twenty feet away,
another monument,
the grave of my brother's nanny.
"She wanted him for her own," mother whispers.
"Now she's got him."

A decade passes.
The game of Cemetery Chess progresses slowly.
Mother dies; her monument
erected midway between brother and nanny.
As we lower my mother down
I whisper to the nanny:

"Check."

• • •

A Dirge

JOHN WEBSTER

Call for the robin-redbreast and the wren,
Since o'er shady groves they hover,
And with leaves and flowers do cover
The friendless bodies of unburied men.
Call unto his funeral dole
The ant, the field-mouse, and the mole,
To rear him hillocks that shall keep him warm,
And (when gay tombs are robb'd) sustain no harm;
    But keep the wolf far thence, that's foe to men,
    For with his nails he'll dig them up again.

• • •

Oil and Blood

W.B. YEATS

In tombs of gold and lapis lazuli
Bodies of holy men and women exude
Miraculous oil, odour of violet.
But under heavy loads of trampled clay
Lie bodies of the vampires full of blood;
Their shrouds are bloody and their lips are wet.

. . .

"Safe in their alabaster chambers"

EMILY DICKINSON

Safe in their alabaster chambers,
Untouched by morning and untouched by noon,
Sleep the meek members of the resurrection,
Rafter of satin, and roof of stone.

Light laughs the breeze in her castle of sunshine;
Babbles the bee in a stolid ear;
Pipe the sweet birds in ignorant cadence,—
Ah, what sagacity perished here!

Grand go the years in the crescent above them;
Worlds scoop their arcs, and firmaments row,
Diadems drop and Doges surrender,
Soundless as dots on a disk of snow.

. . .

The Grave of Shelley

OSCAR WILDE

Like burnt-out torches by a sick man's bed
    Gaunt cypress-trees stand round the sun-bleached stone;
    Here doth the little night-owl make her throne,
And the slight lizard show his jewelled head.
And, where the chaliced poppies flame to red,
    In the still chamber of yon pyramid
    Surely some Old-World Sphinx lurks darkly hid,
Grim warder of this pleasaunce of the dead.

Ah! sweet indeed to rest within the womb
    Of Earth, great mother of eternal sleep,
But sweeter far for thee a restless tomb
    In the blue cavern of an echoing deep,
Or where the tall ships founder in the gloom
    Against the rocks of some wave-shattered steep.

• • •

O Earth! Art Thou Not Weary

JULIA C. R. DORR

O Earth! art thou not weary of thy graves?
Dear patient mother Earth, upon thy breast
How are they heaped from farthest east to west!
From the dim north, where the wild storm-wind raves
O'er the cold surge that chills the shore it laves,
To sunlit isles by softest seas caressed,
Where roses bloom alway and song-birds nest,
How thick they lie—like flocks upon the waves!
There is no mountain-top so far and high,
No desert so remote, no vale so deep,
No spot by man so long untenanted,

But the pale moon, slow marching up the sky,
Sees over some lone grave the shadows creep!
O Earth! art thou not weary of thy dead?

. . .

In the Cemetery

THOMAS HARDY

"You see those mothers squabbling there?"
Remarks the man of the cemetery.
"One says in tears, *'Tis mine lies here!'*
Another, *'Nay mine, you Pharisee!'*
Another, *'How dare you move my flowers*
And put your own on this grave of ours!'
But all their children were laid therein
At different times, like sprats in a tin.
"And then the main drain had to cross,
And we moved the lost some nights ago,
And packed them away in the general foss
With hundreds more. But their folks don't know,
And as well cry over a new-laid drain
As anything else, to ease your pain!"

. . .

The City Dead-House

WALT WHITMAN

By the city dead-house by the gate,
As idly sauntering wending my way from the clangor,
I curious pause, for lo, an outcast form, a poor dead prostitute brought,
Her corpse they deposit unclaim'd, it lies on the damp brick pavement,
The divine woman, her body, I see the body, I look on it alone,
That house once full of passion and beauty, all else I notice not,

Nor stillness so cold, nor running water from faucet, nor odors morbific
  impress me,
But the house alone—that wondrous house—that delicate fair house—
  that ruin!
That immortal house more than all the rows of dwellings ever built!
Or white-domed capitol with majestic figure surmounted, or all the old
  high-spired cathedrals,
That little house alone more than them all—poor, desperate house!
Fair, fearful wreck—tenement of a soul—itself a soul,
Unclaim'd, avoided house—take one breath from my tremulous lips,
Take one tear dropt aside as I go for thought of you,
Dead house of love—house of madness and sin, crumbled, crush'd,
House of life, erewhile talking and laughing—but ah, poor house, dead
  even then,
Months, years, an echoing, garnish'd house—but dead, dead, dead.

• • •

From "Tract"

WILLIAM CARLOS WILLIAMS

I will teach you my townspeople
how to perform a funeral —
for you have it over a troop
of artists—
unless one should scour the world —
you have the ground sense necessary.

See! the hearse leads.
I begin with a design for a hearse.
For Christ's sake not black —
nor white either — and not polished!
Let it be weathered — like a farm wagon —
with gilt wheels (this could be
applied fresh at small expense)
or no wheels at all:
a rough dray to drag over the ground.

Knock the glass out!
My God—glass,   my townspeople!
For what purpose?   Is it for the dead
to look out or   for us to see
how well he is housed   or to see
the flowers or   the lack of them —
or what?
To keep the rain   and snow from him?
He will have a   heavier rain soon:
pebbles and dirt   and what not.
Let there be no glass —
and no upholstery   phew!
and no little   brass rollers
and small easy wheels   on the bottom —
my townspeople   what are you thinking of?

• • •

A Question

JOHN MILLINGTON SYNGE

I ask'd if I got sick and died, would you
With my black funeral go walking too,
If you'd stand close to hear them talk or pray
While I'm let down in that steep bank of clay.

And, No, you said, for if you saw a crew
Of living idiots pressing round that new
Oak coffin—they alive, I dead beneath
That board—you'd rave and rend them with your teeth.

• • •

Finnegan's Wake

TRADITIONAL IRISH DRINKING SONG

Tim Finnegan lived in Walkin Street, a gentle Irishman mighty odd
He had a brogue both rich and sweet, an' to rise in the world he carried a
    hod
You see he'd a sort of a tipplers way but the love for the liquor poor Tim was
    born
To help him on his way each day, he'd a drop of the craythur every morn

Whack fol the dah now dance to yer partner around the flure yer trotters
    shake
    Wasn't it the truth I told you? Lots of fun at Finnegan's Wake

One morning Tim got rather full, his head felt heavy which made him
    shake
Fell from a ladder and he broke his skull, and they carried him home his
    corpse to wake
Rolled him up in a nice clean sheet, and laid him out upon the bed
A bottle of whiskey at his feet and a barrel of porter at his head

His friends assembled at the wake, and Mrs Finnegan called for lunch
First she brought in tay and cake, then pipes, tobacco and whiskey punch
Biddy O'Brien began to cry, "Such a nice clean corpse, did you ever see,
Tim avourneen, why did you die?", "Will ye hould your gob?" said Paddy
    McGee

Then Maggie O'Connor took up the job, "Biddy," says she, "you're
    wrong, I'm sure."
Biddy gave her a belt in the gob and left her sprawling on the floor
Then the war did soon engage, t'was woman to woman and man to man
Shillelagh law was all the rage and a row and a ruction soon began

Mickey Maloney ducked his head when a bucket of whiskey flew at him
It missed, and falling on the bed, the liquor scattered over Tim
Bedad he revives, see how he rises, Timothy rising from the bed,
Saying, "Whittle your whiskey around like blazes, t'underin' Jaysus, do ye
    think I'm dead?"

Whack fol the dah now dance to yer partner around the flure yer trotters shake
   Wasn't it the truth I told you? Lots of fun at Finnegan's Wake

•   •   •

From "Tetélestai"

CONRAD AIKEN

How shall we praise the magnificence of the dead,
The great man humbled, the haughty brought to dust?
Is there a horn we should not blow as proudly
For the meanest of us all, who creeps his days,
Guarding his heart from blows, to die obscurely?
I am no king, have laid no kingdoms waste,
Taken no princes captive, led no triumphs
Of weeping women through long walls of trumpets;
Say rather I am no one, or an atom;
Say rather, two great gods in a vault of starlight
Play ponderingly at chess; and at the game's end
One of the pieces, shaken, falls to the floor
And runs to the darkest corner; and that piece
Forgotten there, left motionless, is I . . . .
Say that I have no name, no gifts, no power,
Am only one of millions, mostly silent;
One who came with lips and hands and a heart,
Looked on beauty, and loved it, and then left it.
Say that the fates of time and space obscured me,
Led me a thousand ways to pain, bemused me,
Wrapped me in ugliness; and like great spiders
Dispatched me at their leisure. . . . Well, what then?
Should I not hear, as I lie down in dust,
The horns of glory blowing above my burial?

•   •   •

what comes next

In which the poets offer their best guesses about the afterlife (or lack thereof)

The Death Secret

ROBERT BLAIR

Tell us, ye dead! will none of you in pity
To those you left behind disclose the secret?
O! that some courteous ghost would blab it out
What 'tis you are, and we must shortly be.
I've heard that souls departed have sometimes
Forewarn'd men of their death. 'Twas kindly done
To knock and give th' alarm. But what means
This stinted charity? 'Tis but lame kindness
That does its work by halves. Why might you not
Tell us what 'tis to die? Do the strict laws
Of your society forbid your speaking
Upon a point so nice? I'll ask no more.
Sullen, like lamps in sepulchres, your shine
Enlightens but yourselves. Well 'tis no matter:
A very little time will clear up all,
And make us learn'd as you are, and as close.

• • •

To a Dead Man

CARL SANDBURG

Over the dead line we have called to you
To come across with a word to us,
Some beaten whisper of what happens
Where you are over the dead line
Deaf to our calls and voiceless.

The flickering shadows have not answered
Nor your lips sent a signal
Whether love talks and roses grow
And the sun breaks at morning
Splattering the sea with crimson.

• • •

Bring Them Not Back

JAMES BENJAMIN KENYON

Yet, O my friend—pale conjurer, I call
Thee friend—bring, bring the dead not back again,
Since for the tears, the darkness and the pain
Of unrequited friendship—for the gall
That hatred mingles with fond love—for all
Life's endless turmoil, bitterness and bane,
Thou hast given dreamless rest. Still let the rain,
And sunshine, and the dews from heaven fall
Upon the graves of those whose peaceful eyes
Thy breath hath sealed forever. Let the song
Of summer birds be theirs, and in the skies
Let the pale stars keep vigil all night long.
O death, call not the holy dead to rise,
Again to feel the cold world's ruth and wrong.

• • •

"You may bury me in de East"

TRADITIONAL SLAVE SONG (US)

You may bury me in de East,
  You may bury me in de West,
   But I'll hear de trumpet sound
    In-a dat mornin'.
I know de moonlight, I know de starlight;
 I lay dis body down.
I walk in de moonlight, I walk in de starlight;
 I lay dis body down.
I know de graveyard, I know de graveyard,
  When I lay dis body down.
I walk in de graveyard, I walk troo de graveyard
  To lay dis body down.

I lay in de grave an' stretch out my arms;
  I lay dis body down.
I go to de judgment in de evenin' of de day
  When I lay dis body down.
An' my soul an' yo' soul will meet in de day
  When I lay dis body down.

• • •

From *Troas*

SENECA

After Death nothing is, and nothing Death;
The utmost limits of a gasp of breath.
Let the ambitious zealot lay aside
His hope of heav'n; (whose faith is but his pride)
Let slavish souls lay by their fear,
Nor be concern'd which way, or where,
After this life they shall be hurl'd:
Dead, we become the lumber of the world;
And to that mass of matter shall be swept,
Where things destroy'd with things unborn are kept;
Devouring time swallows us whole,
Impartial Death confounds body and soul.
For Hell, and the foul Fiend that rules
    The everlasting fiery goals,
Devis'd by rogues, dreaded by fools,
With his grim griesly dog that keeps the door,
    Are senseless stories, idle tales,
Dreams, whimsies, and no more.

Translated from the Latin by John Wilmot, Earl of Rochester

• • •

"Against the Fear of Death"
(from *On the Nature of Things*)

LUCRETIUS

What has this Bugbear Death to frighten Man,
If Souls can die, as well as Bodies can?
For, as before our Birth we felt no Pain,
When Punique arms infested Land and Main,
When Heaven and Earth were in confusion hurl'd,
For the debated Empire of the World,
Which aw'd with dreadful expectation lay,
Sure to be Slaves, uncertain who shou'd sway:
So, when our mortal frame shall be disjoyn'd,
The lifeless Lump uncoupled from the mind,
From sense of grief and pain we shall be free;
We shall not feel, because we shall not *Be*.

*

For whosoe'r shall in misfortunes live,
Must *Be*, when those misfortunes shall arrive;
And since the Man who *Is* not, feels not woe,
(For death exempts him and wards off the blow,
Which we, the living, only feel and bear)
What is there left for us in Death to fear?
When once that pause of life has come between,
'Tis just the same as we had never been.
And therefore if a Man bemoan his lot,
That after death his mouldring limbs shall rot,
Or flames, or jaws, of Beasts devour his Mass,
Know, he's an unsincere, unthinking Ass.

Translated from the Latin by John Dryden

• • •

1 Corinthians 15:51–57

KING JAMES VERSION

Behold, I shew you a mystery; We shall not all sleep, but we shall all be
  changed,
In a moment, in the twinkling of an eye, at the last trump: for the
  trumpet shall sound, and the dead shall be raised incorruptible, and
  we shall be changed.
For this corruptible must put on incorruption, and this mortal must put
  on immortality.
So when this corruptible shall have put on incorruption, and this mortal
  shall have put on immortality, then shall be brought to pass the saying
  that is written, Death is swallowed up in victory.
O death, where is thy sting? O grave, where is thy victory?
The sting of death is sin; and the strength of sin is the law.
But thanks be to God, which giveth us the victory through our Lord
  Jesus Christ.

• • •

From *In Memoriam*

ALFRED, LORD TENNYSON

Do we indeed desire the dead
Should still be near us at our side?
Is there no baseness we would hide?
No inner vileness that we dread?

Shall he for whose applause I strove,
I had such reverence for his blame,
See with clear eye some hidden shame
And I be lessen'd in his love?

I wrong the grave with fears untrue:
Shall love be blamed for want of faith?
There must be wisdom with great Death:
The dead shall look me thro' and thro'.

Be near us when we climb or fall:
Ye watch, like God, the rolling hours
With larger other eyes than ours,
To make allowance for us all.

. . .

From *The Odyssey*

HOMER

[Odysseus descends into the Underworld]

"When lo! appear'd along the dusky coasts,
Thin, airy shoals of visionary ghosts:
Fair, pensive youths, and soft enamour'd maids;
And wither'd elders, pale and wrinkled shades;
Ghastly with wounds the forms of warriors slain
Stalk'd with majestic port, a martial train:
These and a thousand more swarm'd o'er the ground,
And all the dire assembly shriek'd around.
Astonish'd at the sight, aghast I stood,
And a cold fear ran shivering through my blood;
Straight I command the sacrifice to haste,
Straight the flay'd victims to the flames are cast,
And mutter'd vows, and mystic song applied
To grisly Pluto, and his gloomy bride."

. . .

"Curious to view the kings of ancient days,
The mighty dead that live in endless praise,
Resolved I stand; and haply had survey'd
The godlike Theseus, and Pirithous' shade;
But swarms of spectres rose from deepest hell,
With bloodless visage, and with hideous yell.
They scream, they shriek; and groans and dismal sounds
Stun my scared ears, and pierce hell's utmost bounds.

No more my heart the dismal din sustains,
And my cold blood hangs shivering in my veins;
Lest Gorgon, rising from the infernal lakes,
With horrors arm'd, and curls of hissing snakes,
Should fix me stiffen'd at the monstrous sight,
A stony image, in eternal night!
Straight from the direful coast to purer air
I speed my flight, and to my mates repair.
My mates ascend the ship; they strike their oars;
The mountains lessen, and retreat the shores;
Swift o'er the waves we fly; the freshening gales
Sing through the shrouds, and stretch the swelling sails."

Translated from the Greek by Alexander Pope

. . .

How I Walked Alone in the Jungles of Heaven

VACHEL LINDSAY

Oh, once I walked in Heaven, all alone
Upon the sacred cliffs above the sky.
God and the angels, and the gleaming saints
Had journeyed out into the stars to die.

They had gone forth to win far citizens,
Bought at great price, bring happiness for all:
By such a harvest make a holier town
And put new life within old Zion's wall.

Each chose a far-off planet for his home,
Speaking of love and mercy, truth and right,
Envied and cursed, thorn-crowned and scourged in time,
Each tasted death on his appointed night.

Then resurrection day from sphere to sphere
Sped on, with all the POWERS arisen again,
While with them came in clouds recruited hosts
Of sun-born strangers and of earth-born men.

And on that day gray prophet saints went down
And poured atoning blood upon the deep,
Till every warrior of old Hell flew free
And all the torture fires were laid asleep.

And Hell's lost company I saw return
Clear-eyed, with plumes of white, the demons bold
Climbed with the angels now on Jacob's stair,
And built a better Zion than the old.

*

And yet I walked alone on azure cliffs
A lifetime long, and loved each untrimmed vine:
The rotted harps, the swords of rusted gold,
The jungles of all Heaven then were mine.
Oh mesas and throne-mountains that I found!
Oh strange and shaking thoughts that touched me there,
Ere I beheld the bright returning wings
That came to spoil my secret, silent lair!

•   •   •

The City in the Sea

EDGAR ALLAN POE

Lo! Death has reared himself a throne
In a strange city lying alone
Far down within the dim West,
Where the good and the bad and the worst and the best
Have gone to their eternal rest.
There shrines and palaces and towers
(Time-eaten towers that tremble not!)
Resemble nothing that is ours.
Around, by lifting winds forgot,
Resignedly beneath the sky
The melancholy waters lie.

No rays from the holy heaven come down
On the long night-time of that town;
But light from out the lurid sea
Streams up the turrets silently —
Gleams up the pinnacles far and free —
Up domes — up spires — up kingly halls —
Up fanes — up Babylon-like walls —
Up shadowy long-forgotten bowers
Of sculptured ivy and stone flowers —
Up many and many a marvellous shrine
Whose wréathed friezes intertwine
The viol, the violet, and the vine.
Resignedly beneath the sky
The melancholy waters lie.
So blend the turrets and shadows there
That all seem pendulous in air,
While from a proud tower in the town
Death looks gigantically down.

There open fanes and gaping graves
Yawn level with the luminous waves;
But not the riches there that lie
In each idol's diamond eye —
Not the gaily-jewelled dead
Tempt the waters from their bed;
For no ripples curl, alas!
Along that wilderness of glass —
No swellings tell that winds may be
Upon some far-off happier sea —
No heavings hint that winds have been
On seas less hideously serene.

But lo, a stir is in the air!
The wave — there is a movement there!
As if the towers had thrown aside,
In slightly sinking, the dull tide —
As if their tops had feebly given
A void within the filmy Heaven.
The waves have now a redder glow —
The hours are breathing faint and low —
And when, amid no earthly moans,
Down, down that town shall settle hence,
Hell, rising from a thousand thrones,
Shall do it reverence.

• • •

The Dead Man Walking

THOMAS HARDY

They hail me as one living,
  But don't they know
That I have died of late years,
  Untombed although?

I am but a shape that stands here,
  A pulseless mould,
A pale past picture, screening
  Ashes gone cold.

Not at a minute's warning,
  Not in a loud hour,
For me ceased Time's enchantments
  In hall and bower.

There was no tragic transit,
  No catch of breath,
When silent seasons inched me
  On to this death . . .

— A Troubadour-youth I rambled
  With Life for lyre,
The beats of being raging
  In me like fire.

But when I practised eyeing
  The goal of men,
It iced me, and I perished
  A little then.

When passed my friend, my kinsfolk,
  Through the Last Door,
And left me standing bleakly,
  I died yet more;

And when my Love's heart kindled
    In hate of me,
Wherefore I knew not, died I
    One more degree.

And if when I died fully
    I cannot say,
And changed into the corpse-thing
    I am to-day,

Yet is it that, though whiling
    The time somehow
In walking, talking, smiling,
    I live not now.

• • •

The Dance of Death

JOHANN WOLFGANG VON GOETHE

The warder looks down at the mid hour of night,

On the tombs that lie scatter'd below:
The moon fills the place with her silvery light,

And the churchyard like day seems to glow.
When see! first one grave, then another opes wide,
And women and men stepping forth are descried,

In cerements snow-white and trailing.

In haste for the sport soon their ankles they twitch,

And whirl round in dances so gay;
The young and the old, and the poor, and the rich,

But the cerements stand in their way;

And as modesty cannot avail them aught here,
They shake themselves all, and the shrouds soon appear

Scatter'd over the tombs in confusion.

Now waggles the leg, and now wriggles the thigh,

As the troop with strange gestures advance,
And a rattle and clatter anon rises high,

As of one beating time to the dance.
The sight to the warder seems wondrously queer,
When the villainous Tempter speaks thus in his ear:

"Seize one of the shrouds that lie yonder!"

Quick as thought it was done! and for safety he fled

Behind the church-door with all speed;
The moon still continues her clear light to shed

On the dance that they fearfully lead.
But the dancers at length disappear one by one,
And their shrouds, ere they vanish, they carefully don,

And under the turf all is quiet.

But one of them stumbles and shuffles there still,

And gropes at the graves in despair;
Yet 'tis by no comrade he's treated so ill

The shroud he soon scents in the air.
So he rattles the door—for the warder 'tis well
That 'tis bless'd, and so able the foe to repel,

All cover'd with crosses in metal.

The shroud he must have, and no rest will allow,

There remains for reflection no time;
On the ornaments Gothic the wight seizes now,

And from point on to point hastes to climb.
Alas for the warder! his doom is decreed!
Like a long-legged spider, with ne'er-changing speed,

Advances the dreaded pursuer.

The warder he quakes, and the warder turns pale,

The shroud to restore fain had sought;
When the end,—now can nothing to save him avail,—

In a tooth formed of iron is caught.
With vanishing lustre the moon's race is run,
When the bell thunders loudly a powerful One,

And the skeleton fails, crush'd to atoms.

Translated from the German by Edgar Alfred Bowring

• • •

"The only ghost I ever saw"

EMILY DICKINSON

The only ghost I ever saw
Was dressed in mechlin,—so;
He wore no sandal on his foot,
And stepped like flakes of snow.
His gait was soundless, like the bird,
But rapid, like the roe;
His fashions quaint, mosaic,
Or, haply, mistletoe.
His conversation seldom,
His laughter like the breeze

That dies away in dimples
Among the pensive trees.
Our interview was transient,—
Of me, himself was shy;
And God forbid I look behind
Since that appalling day!

• • •

From Generation to Generation

WILLIAM DEAN HOWELLS

Innocent spirits, bright, immaculate ghosts!
Why throng your heavenly hosts,
As eager for their birth
In this sad home of death, this sorrow-haunted earth?

Beware! Beware! Content you where you are,
And shun this evil star,
Where we who are doomed to die
Have our brief being, and pass, we know not where or why.

We have not to consent or to refuse;
It is not ours to choose:
We come because we must,
We know not by what law, if unjust or if just.

The doom is on us, as it is on you,
That nothing can undo;
And all in vain you warn:
As your fate is to die, our fate is to be born.

• • •

When Coldness Wraps This Suffering Clay

LORD BYRON

When coldness wraps this suffering clay,
    Ah! whither strays the immortal mind?
It cannot die, it cannot stay,
    But leaves its darken'd dust behind.
Then, unembodied, doth it trace
    By steps each planet's heavenly way?
Or fill at once the realms of space,
    A thing of eyes, that all survey?

Eternal, boundless, undecay'd,
    A thought unseen, but seeing all,
All, all in earth or skies display'd,
    Shall it survey, shall it recall:
Each fainter trace that memory holds
    So darkly of departed years,
In one broad glance the soul beholds,
    And all, that was, at once appears.

Before Creation peopled earth,
    Its eye shall roll through chaos back;
And where the farthest heaven had birth,
    The spirit trace its rising track.
And where the future mars or makes,
    Its glance dilate o'er all to be,
While sun is quench'd or system breaks,
    Fix'd in its own eternity.

Above or Love, Hope, Hate, or Fear,
    It lives all passionless and pure:
An age shall fleet like earthly year;
    Its years as moments shall endure.
Away, away, without a wing,
    O'er all, through all, its thought shall fly,
A nameless and eternal thing,
    Forgetting what it was to die.

• • •

The Garden of Proserpine

ALGERNON CHARLES SWINBURNE

From too much love of living,
    From hope and fear set free,
We thank with brief thanksgiving
    Whatever gods may be
That no life lives for ever;
That dead men rise up never;
That even the weariest river
    Winds somewhere safe to sea.

Then star nor sun shall waken,
    Nor any change of light:
Nor sound of waters shaken,
    Nor any sound or sight:
Nor wintry leaves nor vernal,
Nor days nor things diurnal;
Only the sleep eternal
    In an eternal night.

• • •

From *Songs of Kabir*

KABIR

The devout seeker is he who mingles in his heart the double currents of love
    and detachment, like the mingling of the streams of Ganges and Jumna;
In his heart the sacred water flows day and night; and thus the round of
    births and deaths is brought to an end.

Behold what wonderful rest is in the Supreme Spirit! and he enjoys it, who
    makes himself meet for it.
Held by the cords of love, the swing of the Ocean of Joy sways to and fro;
    and a mighty sound breaks forth in song.
See what a lotus blooms there without water! and Kabîr says
"My heart's bee drinks its nectar."

What a wonderful lotus it is, that blooms at the heart of the spinning wheel of
the universe! Only a few pure souls know of its true delight.
Music is all around it, and there the heart partakes of the joy of the Infinite Sea.
Kabîr says: "Dive thou into that Ocean of sweetness: thus let all errors of life
and of death flee away."

Behold how the thirst of the five senses is quenched there! and the three forms
of misery are no more!
Kabîr says: "It is the sport of the Unattainable One: look within, and behold
how the moon-beams of that Hidden One shine in you."
There falls the rhythmic beat of life and death:
Rapture wells forth, and all space is radiant with light.
There the Unstruck Music is sounded; it is the music of the love of the three
worlds.
There millions of lamps of sun and of moon are burning;
There the drum beats, and the lover swings in play.
There love-songs resound, and light rains in showers; and the worshipper is
entranced in the taste of the heavenly nectar.
Look upon life and death; there is no separation between them,
The right hand and the left hand are one and the same.
Kabîr says: "There the wise man is speechless; for this truth may never be
found in Vadas or in books."

I have had my Seat on the Self-poised One,
I have drunk of the Cup of the Ineffable,
I have found the Key of the Mystery,
I have reached the Root of Union.
Travelling by no track, I have come to the Sorrowless Land: very easily has the
mercy of the great Lord come upon me.
They have sung of Him as infinite and unattainable: but I in my meditations
have seen Him without sight.
That is indeed the sorrowless land, and none know the path that leads there:
Only he who is on that path has surely transcended all sorrow.
Wonderful is that land of rest, to which no merit can win;
It is the wise who has seen it, it is the wise who has sung of it.
This is the Ultimate Word: but can any express its marvellous savour?
He who has savoured it once, he knows what joy it can give.
Kabîr says: "Knowing it, the ignorant man becomes wise, and the wise man
becomes speechless and silent,

The worshipper is utterly inebriated,
His wisdom and his detachment are made perfect;
He drinks from the cup of the inbreathings and the outbreathings of love."

There the whole sky is filled with sound, and there that music is made
without fingers and without strings;
There the game of pleasure and pain does not cease.
Kabîr says: "If you merge your life in the Ocean of Life, you will find your
life in the Supreme Land of Bliss."

What a frenzy of ecstasy there is in every hour! and the worshipper is pressing
out and drinking the essence of the hours: he lives in the life of Brahma.
I speak truth, for I have accepted truth in life; I am now attached to truth, I
have swept all tinsel away.
Kabîr says: "Thus is the worshipper set free from fear; thus have all errors of
life and of death left him."

There the sky is filled with music:
There it rains nectar:
There the harp-strings jingle, and there the drums beat.
What a secret splendour is there, in the mansion of the sky!
There no mention is made of the rising and the setting of the sun;
In the ocean of manifestation, which is the light of love, day and night are
felt to be one.
Joy for ever, no sorrow,—no struggle!
There have I seen joy filled to the brim, perfection of joy;
No place for error is there.
Kabîr says: "There have I witnessed the sport of One Bliss!"

I have known in my body the sport of the universe: I have escaped from the
error of this world.
The inward and the outward are become as one sky, the Infinite and the
finite are united: I am drunken with the sight of this All!
This Light of Thine fulfils the universe: the lamp of love that burns on the
salver of knowledge.
Kabîr says: "There error cannot enter, and the conflict of life and death is
felt no more."

Translated from the Persian by Rabîndranâth Tagore

• • •

274

The Old Mendicant

THÍCH NHẤT HẠNH

Being rock, being gas, being mist, being Mind,
being the mesons travelling among the galaxies
at the speed of light,
you have come here, my beloved.
And your blue eyes shine, so beautiful, so deep.
You have taken the path traced for you
from the non-beginning and the never-ending.
You say that on your way here
you have gone through
many millions of births and deaths.
Innumerable times you have been transformed
into firestorms in outer space.
You have used your own body
to measure the age of the mountains and rivers.
You have manifested yourself
as trees, grass, butterflies, single-celled beings,
and as chrysanthemums.
But the eyes with which you look at me this morning
tell me that you have never died.
Your smile invites me into the game
whose beginning no one knows,
the game of hide-and-seek.

O green caterpillar, you are solemnly using your body
to measure the length of the rose branch that grew last Summer.
Everyone says that you, my beloved, were just born this Spring.
Tell me, how long have you been around?
Why wait until this moment to reveal yourself to me,
carrying with you that smile which is so silent and so deep?
O caterpillar, suns, moons, and stars flow out
each time I exhale.
Who knows that the infinitely large must be found
in your tiny body?
Upon each point on your body,
thousands of Buddha fields have been established.

With each stretch of your body, you measure time
from the non-beginning to the never-ending.
The great mendicant of old is still there on Vulture Peak,
contemplating the ever-splendid sunset.

Gautama, how strange!
Who said that the Udumbara flower blooms
only once every 3,000 years?

The sound of the rising tide—you cannot help hearing it
if you have an attentive ear.

• • •

The To-be-forgotten

THOMAS HARDY

    I heard a small sad sound,
And stood awhile among the tombs around:
"Wherefore, old friends," said I, "are you distrest,
    Now, screened from life's unrest?"

    —"O not at being here;
But that our future second death is near;
When, with the living, memory of us numbs,
    And blank oblivion comes!

    "These, our sped ancestry,
Lie here embraced by deeper death than we;
Nor shape nor thought of theirs can you descry
    With keenest backward eye.

    "They count as quite forgot;
They are as men who have existed not;
Theirs is a loss past loss of fitful breath;
    It is the second death.

"We here, as yet, each day
Are blest with dear recall; as yet, can say
We hold in some soul loved continuance
          Of shape and voice and glance.

"But what has been will be —
First memory, then oblivion's swallowing sea;
Like men foregone, shall we merge into those
          Whose story no one knows.

"For which of us could hope
To show in life that world-awakening scope
Granted the few whose memory none lets die,
          But all men magnify?

"We were but Fortune's sport;
Things true, things lovely, things of good report
We neither shunned nor sought . . . We see our bourne,
          And seeing it we mourn."

•   •   •

From "Oh May I Join the Choir Invisible"

GEORGE ELIOT

May I reach
That purest heaven, be to other souls
The cup of strength in some great agony,
Enkindle generous ardor, feed pure love,
Beget the smiles that have no cruelty—
Be the sweet presence of a good diffused,
And in diffusion ever more intense.
So shall I join the choir invisible
Whose music is the gladness of the world.

•   •   •

"If I shouldn't be alive"

EMILY DICKINSON

If I shouldn't be alive
When the robins come,
Give the one in red cravat
A memorial crumb.

If I couldn't thank you,
Being just asleep,
You will know I'm trying
With my granite lip!

• • •

All Soul's Day

D.H. LAWRENCE

Be careful, then, and be gentle about death.
For it is hard to die, it is difficult to go through
The door, even when it opens.
And the poor dead, when they have left the walled
And silvery city of the now hopeless body
Where are they to go? Oh where are they to go?

They linger in the shadow of the earth.
The earth's long conical shadow is full of souls
That cannot find the way across the sea of change.
Be kind, Oh be kind to your dead
And give them a little encouragement
And help them to build their little ship of death.
For the soul has a long, long journey after death
To the sweet home of pure oblivion.
Each needs a little ship, a little ship
and the proper store of meal for the longest journey.

Oh, from out of your heart
Provide for your dead once more, equip them
Like departing mariners, lovingly.

. . .

In Death

MARY EMILY BRADLEY

How still the room is! But a while ago
The sound of sobbing voices vexed my ears,
And on my face there fell a rain of tears—
I scarce knew why or whence, but now I know.
For this sweet speaking silence, this surcease
Of the dumb, desperate struggle after breath,
This painless consciousness of perfect peace,
Which fills the place of anguish—it is Death!
What folly to have feared it! Not the best
Of all we knew of life can equal this,
Blending in one the sense of utter rest,
The vivid certainty of boundless bliss!
O Death, the loveliness that is in thee,
Could the world know, the world would cease to be.

. . .

No Death

PHILIP BOURKE MARSTON

I saw in dreams a mighty multitude,—
Gather'd, they seem'd, from North, South, East, and West,
And in their looks such horror was exprest
As must forever words of mine elude.
As if transfix'd by grief, some silent stood,
While others wildly smote upon the breast,

And cried out fearfully, "No rest, no rest!"
Some fled, as if by shapes unseen pursued.
Some laugh'd insanely. Others, shrieking, said:
"To think but yesterday we might have died;
For then God had not thundered, 'Death is dead!'"
They gash'd themselves till they with blood were red.
"Answer, O God; take back this curse!" they cried,
But "Death is dead," was all the voice replied.

· · ·

The Instinct Of Hope

JOHN CLARE

Is there another world for this frail dust
To warm with life and be itself again?
Something about me daily speaks there must,
And why should instinct nourish hopes in vain?
'Tis nature's prophesy that such will be,
And everything seems struggling to explain
The close sealed volume of its mystery.
Time wandering onward keeps its usual pace
As seeming anxious of eternity,
To meet that calm and find a resting place.
E'en the small violet feels a future power
And waits each year renewing blooms to bring,
And surely man is no inferior flower
To die unworthy of a second spring?

· · ·

"A death-blow is a life-blow to some"

EMILY DICKINSON

A death-blow is a life-blow to some
Who, till they died, did not alive become;
Who, had they lived, had died, but when
They died, vitality begun.

• • •

The Transmigration of Souls

AGI MISHOL

It's hard for you to believe in reincarnation
but you're willing to try,
considering the alternative.
If only someone would explain
where the souls are, in a city or a town
or a kind of campground,
and how much one can count on a soul
whose entire existence is based on rumor.

I am reading to you from the Tibetan Book of the Dead
about the soul's journey to city or town
or that campground,
how it rises out of the body like a dove.

The Tibetans make you laugh
but never mind.

What interests you is the exact moment when everything ends,
how from this one moment to the next
blood and heart freeze within the body
and everything else goes on as if nothing had happened.

My darling,
you are almost 90 and know

how to distinguish between death and the fear of death.
When you fall asleep in your armchair
a breeze flutters the pages of your book
and puffs onward.

Even you can see a bird,
forget about yourself
and become its flight.

And the pine cone I saw outside,
hard wooden fist,
will relax in the end, and release
seeds to the earth.

What happens later doesn't interest you,
whether to be buried or burned,
it's not your problem,
and yet I see from your foreshortened perspective
you're beginning to paint a new horizon
even if it is Tibet
just for a laugh
and I'm simply holding
the palette.

Translated from the Hebrew by Lisa Katz

• • •

The Day of Judgment

JONATHAN SWIFT

With a whirl of thought oppressed,
I sunk from reverie to rest.
A horrid vision seized my head,
I saw the graves give up their dead!
Jove, armed with terrors, bursts the skies,
And thunder roars and lightning flies!

Amazed, confused, its fate unknown,
The world stands trembling at his throne!
While each pale sinner hangs his head,
Jove, nodding, shook the heavens, and said:
"Offending race of human kind,
By nature, reason, learning, blind;
You who, through frailty, stepped aside;
And you who never fell—through pride:
You who in different sects have shammed,
And come to see each other damned;
(So some folks told you, but they knew
No more of Jove's designs than you)
—The world's mad business now is o'er,
And I resent these pranks no more.
—I to such blockheads set my wit!
I damn such fools!—Go, go, you're bit."

. . .

God Lay Dead in Heaven

STEPHEN CRANE

God lay dead in heaven;
Angels sang the hymn of the end;
Purple winds went moaning,
Their wings drip-dripping
With blood
That fell upon the earth.
It, groaning thing,
Turned black and sank.
Then from the far caverns
Of dead sins
Came monsters, livid with desire.
They fought,
Wrangled over the world,
A morsel.
But of all sadness this was sad —

A woman's arms tried to shield
The head of a sleeping man
From the jaws of the final beast.

. . .

On the Dunes

SARA TEASDALE

If there is any life when death is over,
   These tawny beaches will know much of me,
I shall come back, as constant and as changeful
   As the unchanging, many-colored sea.

If life was small, if it has made me scornful,
   Forgive me; I shall straighten like a flame
In the great calm of death, and if you want me
   Stand on the sea-ward dunes and call my name.

. . .

Dancing with Electrons

WILLIS BARNSTONE

When I pop out of my file and shut down
      unwillingly, meaning crash
forever, don't forget we've emailed
                  intimately and must keep

it up. I'll hear a fly buzzing in my brain
      before I fall, and will change
my address to will@eternity.com.
                  It's easy. Or you can try

bill@hunger.grave. I will read you.
    I may be dust or ash
but my invisible electricity will be dancing
              with electrons to spare.

Do I freak you out? Have faith. Not in miracles
    but in titanium Macs. My switcher
spans life and death, earth and the template
            of heaven. And if we're trashed

hit lunary@hope.fly. Then a new generation
    of friendly operating systems
will zero us though unbound space where we'll dance
            on both sides of Mars.

carpe diem

In which the poets beseech us to live before we die

First Fig

EDNA ST. VINCENT MILLAY

My candle burns at both ends;
  It will not last the night;
But ah, my foes, and oh, my friends—
  It gives a lovely light!

• • •

Death

RAINER MARIA RILKE

Before us great Death stands
Our fate held close within his quiet hands.
When with proud joy we lift Life's red wine
To drink deep of the mystic shining cup
And ecstasy through all our being leaps—
Death bows his head and weeps.

Translated from the German by Jessie Lamont

• • •

To His Coy Mistress

ANDREW MARVELL

Had we but world enough, and time,
This coyness, Lady, were no crime.
We would sit down and think which way
To walk and pass our long love's day.
Thou by the Indian Ganges' side
Shouldst rubies find: I by the tide
Of Humber would complain. I would
Love you ten years before the Flood,
And you should, if you please, refuse
Till the conversion of the Jews.

My vegetable love should grow
Vaster than empires, and more slow;
An hundred years should go to praise
Thine eyes and on thy forehead gaze;
Two hundred to adore each breast;
But thirty thousand to the rest;
An age at least to every part,
And the last age should show your heart;
For, Lady, you deserve this state,
Nor would I love at lower rate.

But at my back I always hear
Time's wingèd chariot hurrying near;
And yonder all before us lie
Deserts of vast eternity.
Thy beauty shall no more be found,
Nor, in thy marble vault, shall sound
My echoing song: then worms shall try
That long preserved virginity,
And your quaint honour turn to dust,
And into ashes all my lust:
The grave's a fine and private place,
But none, I think, do there embrace.

Now therefore, while the youthful hue
Sits on thy skin like morning dew,
And while thy willing soul transpires
At every pore with instant fires,
Now let us sport us while we may,
And now, like amorous birds of prey,
Rather at once our time devour
Than languish in his slow-chapt power.
Let us roll all our strength and all
Our sweetness up into one ball,
And tear our pleasures with rough strife
Thorough the iron gates of life:
Thus, though we cannot make our sun
Stand still, yet we will make him run.

•   •   •

Blue Squills

SARA TEASDALE

How many million Aprils came
    Before I ever knew
How white a cherry bough could be,
    A bed of squills, how blue!

And many a dancing April
    When life is done with me,
Will lift the blue flame of the flower
    And the white flame of the tree.

Oh burn me with your beauty, then,
    Oh hurt me, tree and flower,
Lest in the end death try to take
    Even this glistening hour.

O shaken flowers, O shimmering trees,
    O sunlit white and blue,
Wound me, that I, through endless sleep,
    May bear the scar of you.

•   •   •

The Emperor of Ice-Cream

WALLACE STEVENS

Call the roller of big cigars,
The muscular one, and bid him whip
In kitchen cups concupiscent curds.
Let the wenches dawdle in such dress
As they are used to wear, and let the boys
Bring flowers in last month's newspapers.
Let be be finale of seem.
The only emperor is the emperor of ice-cream.

Take from the dresser of deal,
Lacking the three glass knobs, that sheet
On which she embroidered fantails once
And spread it so as to cover her face.
If her horny feet protrude, they come
To show how cold she is, and dumb.
Let the lamp affix its beam.
The only emperor is the emperor of ice-cream.

• • •

Ode 1.11

HORACE

Strive not, Leuconoe! to know what end
The gods above to me, or you, will send;
Nor with astrologers consult at all,
That you may better know what can befall—
Whether you live more winters, or your last
Be this, which Tuscan waves against rocks do cast;
Be wise! drink freely, and, in so short a space
Do not protracted hopes of life embrace.
While we are talking, envious time does slide;
Seize the day; the next may be denied.

Translated from the Latin by Sir Thomas Hawkins (modernized by the editor)

• • •

Ecclesiastes 9:4–10

KING JAMES VERSION

For to him that is joined to all the living there is hope: for a living dog is
    better than a dead lion.
For the living know that they shall die: but the dead know not any thing,
    neither have they any more a reward; for the memory of them is
    forgotten.

Also their love, and their hatred, and their envy, is now perished; neither have
    they any more a portion for ever in any thing that is done under the sun.
Go thy way, eat thy bread with joy, and drink thy wine with a merry
    heart; for God now accepteth thy works.
Let thy garments be always white; and let thy head lack no ointment.
Live joyfully with the wife whom thou lovest all the days of the life of
    thy vanity, which he hath given thee under the sun, all the days of thy
    vanity: for that is thy portion in this life, and in thy labour which thou
    takest under the sun.
Whatsoever thy hand findeth to do, do it with thy might; for there is no
    work, nor device, nor knowledge, nor wisdom, in the grave, whither
    thou goest.

· · ·

To the Virgins, to Make Much of Time

ROBERT HERRICK

Gather ye rosebuds while ye may,
    Old Time is still a-flying;
And this same flower that smiles today
    Tomorrow will be dying.

The glorious lamp of heaven, the sun,
    The higher he's a-getting,
The sooner will his race be run,
    And nearer he's to setting.

That age is best which is the first,
    When youth and blood are warmer;
But being spent, the worse, and worst
    Times still succeed the former.

Then be not coy, but use your time,
    And while ye may, go marry;
For having lost but once your prime,
    You may forever tarry.

· · ·

Mariposa

EDNA ST. VINCENT MILLAY

Butterflies are white and blue
In this field we wander through.
Suffer me to take your hand.
Death comes in a day or two.

All the things we ever knew
Will be ashes in that hour:
Mark the transient butterfly,
How he hangs upon the flower.

Suffer me to take your hand.
Suffer me to cherish you
Till the dawn is in the sky.
Whether I be false or true,
Death comes in a day or two.

•   •   •

An Argument

THOMAS MOORE

I've oft been told by learned friars,
That wishing and the crime are one,
And Heaven punishes desires
As much as if the deed were done.

If wishing damns us, you and I
Are damned to all our heart's content;
Come, then, at least we may enjoy
Some pleasure for our punishment!

•   •   •

From *The Rubaiyat*

OMAR KHAYYAM

Whether at Naishapur or Babylon,
    Whether the Cup with sweet or bitter run,
    The Wine of Life keeps oozing drop by drop,
    The Leaves of Life keep falling one by one.

A Book of Verses underneath the Bough,
    A Jug of Wine, a Loaf of Bread, — and Thou
    Beside me singing in the Wilderness —
    Oh, Wilderness were Paradise enow!

Some for the Glories of This World; and some
    Sigh for the Prophet's Paradise to come;
    Ah, take the Cash, and let the Promise go,
    Nor heed the rumble of a distant Drum!

Lo! some we loved, the loveliest and best
    That Time and Fate of all their Vintage prest,
    Have drunk their Cup a Round or two before,
    And one by one crept silently to Rest.

Oh, come with old Khayyam, and leave the Wise
    To talk; one thing is certain, that Life flies;
    One thing is certain, and the Rest is Lies;
    The Flower that once has blown forever dies.

Translated from the Persian by Edward FitzGerald

• • •

Intoxication

CHARLES BAUDELAIRE

One must be forever drunken: that is the sole question of importance.
If you would not feel the horrible burden of Time that bruises your
shoulders and bends you to the earth, you must be drunken without
cease. But how? With wine, with poetry, with virtue, with what you
please. But be drunken. And if sometimes, on the steps of a palace, on
the green grass by a moat, or in the dull loneliness of your chamber, you
should waken up, your intoxication already lessened or gone, ask of the
wind, of the wave, of the star, of the bird, of the timepiece; ask of all
that flees, all that sighs, all that revolves, all that sings, all that speaks, ask
of these the hour; and wind and wave and star and bird and timepiece
will answer you: "It is the hour to be drunken! Lest you be the martyred
slaves of Time, intoxicate yourselves, be drunken without cease! With
wine, with poetry, with virtue, or with what you will."

Translated from the French by James Huneker

• • •

An Epitaph

ANDREW MARVELL

Enough; and leave the rest to Fame!
'Tis to commend her, but to name.
Courtship which, living, she declined,
When dead, to offer were unkind:
Nor can the truest wit, or friend,
Without detracting, her commend.

To say—she lived a virgin chaste
In this age loose and all unlaced;
Nor was, when vice is so allowed,
Of virtue or ashamed or proud;
That her soul was on Heaven so bent,
No minute but it came and went;

That, ready her last debt to pay,
She summ'd her life up every day;
Modest as morn, as mid-day bright,
Gentle as evening, cool as night:
—'Tis true; but all too weakly said.
'Twas more significant, she's dead.

• • •

Midnight Oil

EDNA ST. VINCENT MILLAY

Cut if you will, with Sleep's dull knife,
    Each day to half its length, my friend,—
The years that Time takes off *my* life,
    He'll take from off the other end!

• • •

Since I Have Felt the Sense of Death

HELEN HOYT

Since I have felt the sense of death,
    Since I have borne its dread, its fear—
    Oh, how my life has grown more dear
Since I have felt the sense of death!
Sorrows are good, and cares are small,
Since I have known the loss of all.

Since I have felt the sense of death,
    And death forever at my side—
    Oh, how the world has opened wide
Since I have felt the sense of death!
My hours are jewels that I spend,
For I have seen the hours end.

Since I have felt the sense of death,
    Since I have looked on that black night—
    My inmost brain is fierce with light
Since I have felt the sense of death.
O dark, that made my eyes to see!
O death, that gave my life to me!

• • •

The Choice

DANTE GABRIEL ROSSETTI

Eat thou and drink; to-morrow thou shalt die.
    Surely the earth, that's wise being very old,
    Needs not our help. Then loose me, love, and hold
Thy sultry hair up from my face; that I
May pour for thee this golden wine, brim-high,
    Till round the glass thy fingers glow like gold.
    We'll drown all hours: thy song, while hours are toll'd,
Shall leap, as fountains veil the changing sky.

Now kiss, and think that there are really those,
    My own high-bosomed beauty, who increase
        Vain gold, vain lore, and yet might choose our way!
        Through many years they toil; then comes a day
    They die not,—never having lived,—but cease;
And round their narrow lips the mould falls close.

• • •

Drinking Wine on Grave Sweeping Day

KAO CHU

Hillsides north and south are overrun with graves
sweeping rites on Chingming are nothing but a mess
paper ashes fly like snow-white butterflies

tears from broken hearts stain azaleas red
foxes sleep in tombs once the sun goes down
children play in lamplight on the way back home
who has wine this life should drink until they're drunk
no drop has ever reached the ninefold springs below

Translated from the Chinese by Red Pine

• • •

May Day

SARA TEASDALE

A delicate fabric of bird song
    Floats in the air,
The smell of wet wild earth
    Is everywhere.

Red small leaves of the maple
    Are clenched like a hand,
Like girls at their first communion
    The pear trees stand.

Oh I must pass nothing by
    Without loving it much,
The raindrop try with my lips,
    The grass with my touch;

For how can I be sure
    I shall see again
The world on the first of May
    Shining after the rain?

ossuary

In which the poets write of things that don't fit neatly
into any of the other chapters

What We Know of Death by Drowning

NICK LANTZ

1. Josef Mengele Drowns While Swimming at a Beach in Brazil, 1979

His name then: Wolfgang Gerhard.
How easy, slipping on another man's
   skin. Another country, too,

its sun's heat and light
as insistent as a pair
of forceps.

His pants, left crumpled
on the beach, forged papers
and a few hard candies in the pocket.

Where the water
   was shallow, he could look
   down and see

his shadow passing over
the pale sand, a wobbly twin,

   matching him
stroke for stroke for stroke.

2. Li Po Drowns Trying to Embrace the Reflection of the Moon
   in the Yangtze, 762

The moon is no drinker of wine, so I must
compensate. Surely you've heard

the crows and nightingales
egging me on? The day has dispersed
from the courtyards like a gang
   of sparrows, and nothing

is left of the world that is not
pecked-over, hard and dark
    as the dream of an apple seed.

The young men laugh
at an old man drinking
alone, but here

are my companions:
    my shadow, as loyal
    and thin as a starved dog,

and the moon, his whole face
    wrinkling with laughter.

3. Bob, the Circus Seal, Drowns Himself in His Tank in Galveston, 1911

By then his teeth had rotted out,
    and he often turned to his owner
with his mouth open as if about

to speak, a ruined smell
jetting from inside.

He had already attempted it,

    three days before,
but his owner dove in and pulled him up
onto the slimy planks. His circus show days

were long gone. Sure, some afternoons
a kid might walk by
    and see the scabby painting

on the side of the building: the hoop,
the pedestal, the ghost
of a man in a top hat,

the striped ball now like a clot
of pus streaked
with blood, hovering

over the sleek, dark head.

4. Natalie Wood Drowns under Mysterious Circumstances near
   Santa Catalina Island, 1981

Let me tell you: death
    is a long silk glove
dropped to the floor.

It doesn't remember the heft
of the arm, the fingers
    dancing.

That limb is gone, and nothing
will hold its shape again.

You twirl your pastel skirt. You watch
two cars
race toward the cliff,
    and there is nothing

you can do. So many lives
    you've entered
like a room: swooned,

held the prop pistol
to your own face, sang
for the back row.
    But was it your voice?

What was that name
you were born into?
    Natalia Nikolaevna Zakharenko?
What happened to her?

Was she the one
taken, her family butchered, living
another life
among the enemy people?

Was it the morning?
when she stopped scanning
the horizon for rescuers
    that she turned into you?

5. Hippasus of Metapontum Is Drowned at Sea for the Heresy of
    Discovering Irrational Numbers, ca. 500 BCE

His fellow Pythagoreans had already built
a shrine to his memory
    and placed it where

he passed by every day, but he did not take
    the hint. It was on the ship
that they seized him.

God was an integer, firm
as an unripe apricot.
    But weren't there streets
    in the city that wound forever
into the minute darkness?

Weren't there dreams where he met
himself again and again,
without ever seeming to wake?

The sea is incommensurable.
    Each lungful of air
    kept dividing itself, even as the boat

became a decimal point on the far horizon.

6. Bennie Wint, 20 Years after Faking His Drowning Death, is
   Discovered Alive, 2009

In the first years after I disappeared, I read
every report of drowning: children,

mostly boys,
mostly in their bathtubs,
mostly accidents.

Old men whose lungs filled with fluid
    while they sat in their armchairs.

Fishermen. Swimmers. Immigrants
crowded onto rafts. Some men,
    their throats seize up,
    and they die without

ever swallowing a drop,
as if they never left the shore.

    Some nights I dreamed
what never happened: I held my drowning

in my palm like a giant pearl.
Some days, standing behind
the cash register of my new life,

I felt my lungs flatten out like a pair
of discarded socks. Did I ever think

of the woman I left on the shore
    as I kicked out
past the last of the breakers?

I won't say.
Here it was: I might have drowned
trying to pretend to. I had to swim
so far out, then mark

a different beach
and swim back

a different man, without knowing
if his strength was enough
    to carry me to shore.

. . .

The Killer

RICHARD M. BERLIN

The poem is a capsule where we wrap up our punishable secrets.
—William Carlos Williams

She was old and fragile
and I was just an intern
charged with guiding her care,
her seeing-eye dog in a city hospital.
When I saw a pulse in her jugular vein
I pressed my stethoscope to her chest—
she inhaled and I heard crackles,
like static on a trooper's radio.

I guessed heart failure.
The answer was pneumonia.

Oh I caught my error the next morning,
dripped in fluids and ampicillin,
but she'd been in bed one day too long,
the clot in her calf broken apart
and trapped in the lattice of her lungs.
I stood by her side, stunned
when her breathing stopped,
and I called the team, barked
orders at the code. And I felt
like a killer cornered on a dead-end street,

cops and canines closing in,
thinking confession, still holding my gun.

• • •

Two poems from *Spoon River Anthology*

EDGAR LEE MASTERS

Hod Putt

Here I lie close to the grave
Of Old Bill Piersol,
Who grew rich trading with the Indians, and who
Afterwards took the bankrupt law
And emerged from it richer than ever
Myself grown tired of toil and poverty
And beholding how Old Bill and other grew in wealth,
Robbed a traveler one night near Proctor's Grove,
Killing him unwittingly while doing so,
For the which I was tried and hanged.
That was my way of going into bankruptcy.
Now we who took the bankrupt law in our respective ways
Sleep peacefully side by side.

The Circuit Judge

Take note, passers-by, of the sharp erosions
Eaten in my head-stone by the wind and rain—
Almost as if an intangible Nemesis or hatred
Were marking scores against me,
But to destroy, and not preserve, my memory.
I in life was the Circuit Judge, a maker of notches,
Deciding cases on the points the lawyers scored,
Not on the right of the matter.
O wind and rain, leave my head-stone alone!
For worse than the anger of the wronged,
The curses of the poor,

306

Was to lie speechless, yet with vision clear,
Seeing that even Hod Putt, the murderer,
Hanged by my sentence,
Was innocent in soul compared with me.

. . .

Moth-Terror

BENJAMIN DE CASSERES

I have killed the moth flying around my night-light; wingless and dead it
    lies upon the floor.
(O who will kill the great Time-Moth that eats holes in my soul and that
    burrows in and through my secretest veils!)
My will against its will, and no more will it fly at my night-light or be
    hidden behind the curtains that swing in the winds.
(But O who will shatter the Change-Moth that leaves me in rags—
    tattered old tapestries that swing in the winds that blow out of
    Chaos!)
Night-Moth, Change-Moth, Time-Moth, eaters of dreams and of me!

. . .

Grotesque

AMY LOWELL

Why do the lilies goggle their tongues at me
When I pluck them;
And writhe, and twist,
And strangle themselves against my fingers,
So that I can hardly weave the garland
For your hair?
Why do they shriek your name
And spit at me
When I would cluster them?
Must I kill them

To make them lie still,
And send you a wreath of lolling corpses
To turn putrid and soft
On your forehead
While you dance?

•   •   •

The Poison Tree

WILLIAM BLAKE

I was angry with my friend:
I told my wrath, my wrath did end.
I was angry with my foe:
I told it not, my wrath did grow.

And I watered it in fears,
Night and morning with my tears;
And I sunned it with smiles,
And with soft deceitful wiles.

And it grew both day and night,
Till it bore an apple bright.
And my foe beheld it shine.
And he knew that it was mine,

And into my garden stole
When the night had veiled the pole;
In the morning glad I see
My foe outstretched beneath the tree.

•   •   •

A limerick

EDWARD LEAR

There was an Old Man of Cape Horn,
Who wished he had never been born;
So he sat on a Chair till he died of despair,
That dolorous Man of Cape Horn.

author index

title index

first line index

acknowledgments

Big thanks of a personal nature are due to my parents, Ruthanne & Derek, Terrence & Huxley, Darrell, Billy Dale, my Chicago family, Christine, Songtruth, the L's, Rebecca & Tim, Liz & Bryan, Christy & Jeff, Dan Simon, Veronica Liu, Phyllis, Lois, Mary, Hawk, Z.

I bow to Gary Baddeley at Disinfo, and Jan Johnson, Michael Kerber, Kim Ehart, Kat Salazar, Vanessa Ta, Michael Alexander, and everyone else at Red Wheel/Weiser for believing in this project.

Merci beaucoup to everyone at the University of Arizona's amazing Poetry Center, where I discovered lots of the poems included here.

A very special thank you goes to Frederick T. Courtright of the Permissions Company. Without his generosity and hard work, this anthology would not be what it is.

Thank you to all the poets for putting pen to paper.

And much respect to everyone who has died.

credits & permissions

Paula Gunn Allen, "Something Fragile, Broken" from *Skin and Bones: Poems 1979–1987.* Copyright ©1988 by Paula Gunn Allen. Reprinted with the permission of The Permissions Company, Inc., on behalf of West End Press, Albuquerque, New Mexico, *www.westendpress.org.*

Mary Jo Bang, "Ode to History" from *Elegy.* Copyright © 2007 by Mary Jo Bang. Reprinted with the permission of The Permissions Company, Inc., on behalf of Graywolf Press, *www.graywolfpress.org.*

Willis Barnstone, "Dancing With Electrons" and "Coffins of Black" from *Life Watch.* Copyright ©2004 by Willis Barnstone. Reprinted with the permission of The Permissions Company, Inc., on behalf of BOA Editions, Ltd., *www.boaeditions.org.*

Miranda Beeson, "Flight" from *Poetry After 9/11: An Anthology of New York Poets,* Melville House, 2002 and in the 2011 reissue of the anthology also by Melville House. "Rock Paper Scissors" from *Bateau* 2010. Copyright ©2002 and 2010 by Miranda Beeson. Both reprinted with permission of the author.

Richard M. Berlin, "Dropping the Lamb" and "The Killer" from *Secret Wounds,* BkMk Press (University of Missouri-Kansas City). Copyright ©2011 by Richard M. Berlin. Reprinted with permission of the author and publisher.

Kathleen Sheeder Bonanno, "How to Find Out" and "Homicide Detective" from *Open the Door.* Copyright ©2009 by Kathleen Sheeder Bonanno. Reprinted with the permission of The Permissions Company, Inc. on behalf of Alice James Books, *www. alicejamesbooks.org.*

Laure-Anne Bosselaar, "Stillbirth" from *A New Hunger.* Copyright ©2007 by Laure-Anne Bosselaar. Reprinted with the permission of The Permissions Company, Inc., on behalf of Copper Canyon Press, *www.coppercanyonpress.org.*

David Bottoms, "Under the Vulture Tree" from *Armored Hearts: Selected & New Poems.* Copyright ©1995 by David Bottoms. Reprinted with the permission of The Permissions Company, Inc., on behalf of Copper Canyon Press, *www.coppercanyonpress.org.*

Hayden Carruth, "Testament" from *Toward the Distant Islands: New & Selected Poems.* Copyright ©1996 by Hayden Carruth. Reprinted with the permission of The Permissions Company, Inc., on behalf of Copper Canyon Press, *www.coppercanyonpress.org.*

Kao Chu, "Drinking Wine on Grave Sweeping Day" from *Poems of the Masters: China's Classic Anthology of T'ang and Sung Dynasty Verse,* translated by Red Pine. Copyright © 2003 by Red Pine. Reprinted with the permission of The Permissions Company, Inc. on behalf of Copper Canyon Press, *www.coppercanyonpress.org.*

Lucille Clifton, "after one year," "dying," "oh antic God," "the lost baby poem," and "them bones" from *The Collected Poems of Lucille Clifton.* Copyright ©1987, 2004 by Lucille Clifton. Reprinted with the permission of The Permissions Company, Inc., on behalf of BOA Editions Ltd., *www.boaeditions.org.* "she lived" from *The Book of Light.* Copyright ©1993 by Lucille Clifton. Reprinted with the permission of The Permissions Company, Inc. on behalf of Copper Canyon Press, *www.coppercanyonpress.org.*

Andrei Codrescu, "crepuscular (the family tomb)" and "new orleans limbo" from *Jealous Witness.* Copyright ©2008 by Andrei Codrescu. Reprinted with the permission of The Permissions Company, Inc., on behalf of Coffee House Press, *www.coffeehousepress.org.*

Samantha Cole, "Upon Butchering of the Hog" from *Bigger Than They Appear: Anthology of Very Short Poems,* Accents Publishing, 2011. Copyright ©2011 by Samantha Cole. Reprinted with permission of the author.

Wanda Coleman, "South Central Los Angeles Death Trip, 1982" from *Mercurochrome*, Black Sparrow Press, ©2001 for Wanda Coleman, reprinted with permission of the author.

Billy Collins, "My Number" from *The Apple That Astonished Paris*. Copyright ©1988, 1996 by Billy Collins. Reprinted with the permission of The Permissions Company, Inc., on behalf of the University of Arkansas Press, *www.uapress.com*.

Todd Davis, "Prayer Requests at a Mennonite Church," "Resurrection, or What He Told Me to Do When He Died," and "Some Heaven" from *Some Heaven*, Michigan State University Press. Copyright © 2007 by Todd Davis. Reprinted with permission of the publisher.

Linh Dinh, "Earth Cafeteria" from *All Around What Empties Out*. Copyright ©2003 by Linh Dinh. Reprinted with permission of Tinfish Press and the author.

Alan Dugan, "Funeral Oration for a Mouse," "untitled poem," and "For Euthenasia and Pain-Killing Drugs" from *Poems Seven: New and Complete Poetry*. Copyright ©2001 by Alan Dugan. Reprinted with the permission of The Permissions Company, Inc., on behalf of Seven Stories Press, *www.sevenstories.com*.

Emily Ferrara, "The Difference" and "Mother's Lament" from The Alchemy of Grief, Bordighera Press. Copyright ©2007 by Emily Ferrara. Reprinted with permission of the author.

Nick Flynn, "My Mother Contemplating Her Gun" from *Some Ether*. Copyright ©2000 by Nick Flynn. Reprinted with the permission of The Permissions Company, Inc., on behalf of Graywolf Press, *www.graywolfpress.org*. "Statuary" from *Blind Huber*. Copyright © 2002 by Nick Flynn. Reprinted with the permission of The Permissions Company, Inc., on behalf of Graywolf Press, *www.graywolfpress.org*.

Sarah Freligh, "The Class of '69." Copyright © 2013 by Sarah Freligh. Reprinted with permission of the author.

Barry Gifford, "North Beach Chinese Sonnet" and "Faded Love" from *Imagining Paradise: New and Selected Poems*. Copyright © 2012 by Barry Gifford. Reprinted with the permission of The Permissions Company, Inc., on behalf of Seven Stories Press, *www.sevenstories.com*.

Kimiko Hahn, "Road Kill" from *Killer Verse: Poems of Murder and Mayhem*, Everyman's Library. Copyright © 2011 by Kimiko Hahn. Reprinted with permission of the author.

Linda Hogan, "Affinity: Mustang," "Anatomy," "Call," "The Fox," and "The Given" from *Rounding the Human Corners*. Copyright © 2008 by Linda Hogan. Reprinted with the permission of The Permissions Company, Inc., on behalf of Coffee House Press, *www.coffeehousepress.org*.

Lenore Kandel, "Small Hours Poem" from *Collected Poems of Lenore Kandel*, published by North Atlantic Books. Copyright © 2012 by the Estate of Lenore Kandel. Reprinted with permission of the publisher.

Brigit Pegeen Kelly, "Song" from *Song*. Copyright © 1995 by Brigit Pegeen Kelly. Reprinted with the permission of The Permissions Company, Inc., on behalf of BOA Editions Ltd., *www.boaeditions.org*.

Carol Lynne Knight, "Naming" from *Quantum Entanglement* and *Bigger Than They Appear*. Copyright © 2010 by Carol Lynn Knight. Reprinted with permission of the author.

Nick Lantz, "What We Know of Death by Drowning" from *We Don't Know We Don't Know*. Copyright © 2010 by Nick Lantz. Reprinted with the permission of The Permissions Company, Inc., on behalf of Graywolf Press, *www.graywolfpress.org*.

David Lee, "For Jan, With Love" from *A Legacy of Shadows: Selected Poems*. Copyright © 1999 by David Lee. Reprinted with the permission of The Permissions Company, Inc., on behalf of Copper Canyon Press, *www.coppercanyonpress.org*.

about the editor

Russ Kick is known for his ground-breaking and uniquely informative books, which have sold over half a million copies. He is the editor of the three-volume anthology *The Graphic Canon: The World's Great Literature as Comics and Visuals* (Seven Stories Press). NPR said it is "easily the most ambitious and successfully realized literary project in recent memory," *School Library Journal* called it "startlingly brilliant" and "a masterpiece," and Booklist declared it "a profound work of art." The third volume was a New York *Times* Best Seller.

Russ has also edited the megaselling anthologies *You Are Being Lied To* and *Everything You Know is Wrong*, and has written several nonfiction books, including the cult classic *50 Things You're Not Supposed to Know* (all from The Disinformation Company). The New York *Times* has dubbed him "an information archaeologist," *Details* magazine described him as "a Renaissance man," and *Utne Reader* named him one of its "50 Visionaries Who Are Changing Your World."